Guide to
Math Materials

Guide to
Math Materials

Resources to Support the NCTM Standards

PHYLLIS J.
PERRY

1997
Teacher Ideas Press
A Division of
Libraries Unlimited, Inc.
Englewood, Colorado

Dedicated to
Kimberly Tabor for all of her wonderful
support and advice.

TEACHER IDEAS PRESS
A Division of
Libraries Unlimited, Inc.
P.O. Box 6633
Englewood, CO 80155-6633
(800) 237-6124

Production Editor: Kay Mariea
Copy Editor: Thea De Hart
Proofreader: Eileen Bartlett
Indexer: Nancy Fulton
Typesetter: Kay Minnis

Library of Congress Cataloging-in-Publication Data

Perry, Phyllis J., 1933-
    Guide to math materials : resources to support the NCTM standards /
Phyllis J. Perry.
    xiii, 127 p. 22x28 cm.
    Includes bibliographical references and index.
    ISBN 1-56308-491-0
    1. Mathematics--Study and teaching--Audio-visual aids--Catalogs.
2. Mathematics--Study and teaching (Elementary)--United States.
3. NCTM Standards.   I. Title.
QA18.P47   1997
372.7'044--dc20   96-33101
                                                              CIP

CONTENTS

INTRODUCTION

There have been many calls for reform in the teaching of mathematics, both at the national and local levels. America 2000 and Goals 2000, for example, are national efforts that have called for our students to be "first in the world" in math and science by the year 2000. Boards of education in school districts across the country continually hear requests for "higher academic standards," particularly in the areas of reading, writing, science, and mathematics.

Much of this concern arises because America is increasingly becoming an information society. Calculators, computers, and other technology have greatly affected our way of life. Although it sounds contradictory, technology has made things both easier and more complex for students, teachers, and parents.

Against this background of reform and concern about academic achievement, a dramatic change in the curriculum for the teaching of mathematics has come about since the mid-1980s. Several work groups in the National Council of Teachers of Mathematics (NCTM) addressed this issue,[1] noting that children enter kindergarten with some mathematical experience and understanding and that this understanding deepens if the students are provided with a *developmentally appropriate* curriculum. Such a curriculum encourages exploration and curiosity and allows children time to develop their abilities to solve problems, reason, find connections, and communicate about mathematics.

The work groups further recognized that the mathematics curriculum in kindergarten through fourth grade is vitally important because it establishes the foundation for success at higher grade levels. While it is true that children need to acquire mathematical skills during this time, there is also a qualitative dimension to their learning. How well children come to understand mathematical concepts in the primary grades is very significant, since the beliefs and attitudes about mathematics formed during these years influence a student's thinking, performance, and decisions about further studies of mathematics.

Six basic assumptions were made by the NCTM work groups that governed the selection of the curriculum standards. According to these assumptions the K-4 curriculum should

1) be conceptually oriented,
2) actively involve children in doing mathematics,
3) emphasize the development of children's mathematical thinking and reasoning abilities,
4) emphasize the application of mathematics,
5) include a broad range of content,
6) make appropriate and ongoing use of calculators and computers.[2]

As a result of this work, there are at present 13 curriculum standards for mathematics. Even though these standards are a recent development of work completed since 1986 when the Board of Directors of the National Council of Teachers of Mathematics established the Commission on Standards for School Mathematics, they are not set in stone. In fact, there is already discussion of modifying these standards. Some states have even collapsed the original 13 standards into a smaller number of standards.

Even if the number of standards does change in the coming years, the conceptual framework of the original 13 standards will still provide a strong basis for parents and teachers to consider as they plan mathematical experiences for elementary-aged students. They provide the framework for this book, *Guide to Math Materials*.

This book has two purposes. First, it reinforces the outstanding work done by the National Council of Teachers of Mathematics (NCTM) in developing curriculum standards for students in kindergarten through fourth grade by discussing the 13 strands of mathematics and their implications for teachers and parents who work with children.

Second, it provides some suggested resources within each of these 13 curricular strands that will assist teachers and parents in helping students to enjoy math and to increase their mathematical understandings.

The lists of resources are extensive but by no means exhaustive. They do indicate the range of materials available to parents and teachers. Faced with so many options to choose from, a busy teacher may feel dismayed. Opinions on which products to use are certainly subjective, and only the classroom teacher can make the wisest selection of materials needed for his or her students. To make this list easier to use, the author has marked some items with asterisks (**) to indicate that they are exceptionally good values. For those teachers on a limited budget or who can purchase only a few items, these are the items to buy. Books, manipulatives, games, kits, computer programs, videos, and other items have been included. Computer programs and videos are also marked with special symbols to assist those teachers looking for materials in these newer technologies.

Materials listed in this book are intended to assist teachers and parents of students in kindergarten through fourth grade. Some advanced materials are also included for those teachers who need to challenge fourth-grade students working at a higher academic level.

Each resource has been listed only once, even though many of the materials lend themselves to multiple uses. The author has placed a particular resource in a specific strand knowing that creative teachers and parents may find multiple uses for the same resource and may find it equally valuable or even more valuable in teaching other strands.

Some manipulatives, such as geoboards, tangrams, pattern blocks, and clock faces, are so popular that there simply was not space to list every company that supplies them. When readers need basic, popular items, they should check with a favorite and convenient supplier to see if similar items are available. Prices vary considerably, and the reader may want to check several sources and consider quantity buying to maximize purchasing power.

In some cases, such as with kits containing a variety of manipulatives, the resource was clearly designed to be used across the NCTM standards. To avoid duplication of information, such resources were listed only once, in chapter 14, rather than being included in each chapter.

It should be noted that this book is intended for use as a buyer's guide and not necessarily as a bibliography. This book, therefore, provides information on distributors of books and other items to assist readers who wish to obtain the various items.

Finally, while the author attended conferences and materials exhibits, visited classrooms to observe math lessons in progress and the materials being used, ordered and studied catalogs, and made every effort to be thorough, some excellent math materials were no doubt overlooked. A sufficient number of resources have been included in every standard, however, so that parents and teachers should have a good idea of the variety of materials available.

Following are the 13 standards as published by the National Council of Teachers of Mathematics in the *Curriculum and Evaluation Standards for School Mathematics,* in March 1989.

STANDARD 1: MATHEMATICS AS PROBLEM SOLVING

In grades K-4, the study of mathematics should emphasize problem solving so that students can:

➤ use problem-solving approaches to investigate and understand mathematical content;

➤ formulate problems from everyday mathematical situations;

➤ develop and apply strategies to solve a wide variety of problems;

➤ verify and interpret results with respect to the original problem;

➤ acquire confidence in using mathematics meaningfully.

STANDARD 2: MATHEMATICS AS COMMUNICATION

In grades K-4, the study of mathematics should include numerous opportunities for communication so that students can:

➤ relate physical materials, pictures, and diagrams to mathematical ideas;

➤ reflect on and clarify their thinking about mathematical ideas and situations;

➤ relate their everyday language to mathematical language and symbols;

➤ realize that representing, discussing, reading, writing, and listening to mathematics are a vital part of learning and using mathematics.

STANDARD 3: MATHEMATICS AS REASONING

In grades K-4, the study of mathematics should emphasize reasoning so that students can:

➤ draw logical conclusions about mathematics;

➤ use models, known facts, properties, and relationships to explain their thinking;

➤ justify their answers and solution processes;

➤ use patterns and relationships to analyze mathematical situations;

➤ believe that mathematics makes sense.

STANDARD 4: MATHEMATICAL CONNECTIONS

In grades K-4, the study of mathematics should include opportunities to make connections so that students can:

➤ link conceptual and procedural knowledge;

➤ relate various representations of concepts or procedures to one another;

➤ recognize relationships among different topics in mathematics;

➤ use mathematics in other curriculum areas;

➤ use mathematics in their daily lives.

STANDARD 5: ESTIMATION

In grades K-4, the curriculum should include estimation so students can:

➤ explore estimation strategies;

➤ recognize when an estimate is appropriate;

➤ determine the reasonableness of results;

➤ apply estimation in working with quantities, measurements, computation, and problem solving.

STANDARD 6: NUMBER SENSE AND NUMERATION

In grades K-4, the curriculum should include whole number concepts and skills so that students can:

➤ construct number meanings through real-world experiences and the use of physical materials;

➤ understand our numeration system by relating counting, grouping, and place-value concepts;

➤ develop number sense;

➤ interpret the multiple uses of numbers encountered in the real world.

STANDARD 7: CONCEPTS OF WHOLE NUMBER OPERATIONS

In grades K-4, the mathematics curriculum should include concepts of addition, subtraction, multiplication, and division of whole numbers so that students can:

➤ develop meaning for the operations by modeling and discussing a rich variety of problem situations;

➤ relate the mathematical language and symbolism of operations to problem situations and informal language;

➤ recognize that a wide variety of problem structures can be represented by a single operation;

➤ develop operation sense.

STANDARD 8: WHOLE NUMBER COMPUTATION

In grades K-4, the mathematics curriculum should develop whole number computation so that students can:

➤ model, explain, and develop reasonable proficiency with basic facts and algorithms;

➤ use a variety of mental computation and estimation techniques;

➤ use calculators in appropriate computational situations;

➤ select and use computation techniques appropriate to specific problems and determine whether the results are reasonable.

STANDARD 9: GEOMETRY AND SPATIAL SENSE

In grades K-4, the mathematics curriculum should include two- and three-dimensional geometry so that students can:

➤ describe, model, draw, and classify shapes;

➤ investigate and predict the results of combining, subdividing, and changing shapes;

➤ develop spatial sense;

➤ relate geometric ideas to number and measurement ideas;

➤ recognize and appreciate geometry in their world.

STANDARD 10: MEASUREMENT

In grades K-4, the mathematics curriculum should include measurement so that students can:

➤ understand the attributes of length, capacity, weight, mass, area, volume, time, temperature, and angle;

➤ develop the process of measuring and concepts related to units of measurement;

➤ make and use estimates of measurement;

➤ make and use measurements in problem and everyday situations.

STANDARD 11: STATISTICS AND PROBABILITY

In grades K-4, the mathematics curriculum should include experiences with data analysis and probability so that students can:

➤ collect, organize, and describe data;

➤ construct, read, and interpret displays of data;

➤ formulate and solve problems that involve collecting and analyzing data;

➤ explore concepts of chance.

STANDARD 12: FRACTIONS AND DECIMALS

In grades K-4, the mathematics curriculum should include fractions and decimals so that students can:

➤ develop concepts of fractions, mixed numbers, and decimals;

➤ develop number sense for fractions and decimals;

➤ use models to relate fractions to decimals and to find equivalent fractions;

➤ use models to explore operations on fractions and decimals;

➤ apply fractions and decimals to problem situations.

STANDARD 13: PATTERNS AND RELATIONSHIPS

In grades K-4, the mathematics curriculum should include the study of patterns and relationships so that students can:

➤ recognize, describe, extend, and create a wide variety of patterns;

➤ represent and describe mathematical relationships;

➤ explore the use of variables and open sentences to express relationships.

A chapter of this book has been devoted to each of these standards. Each chapter includes a brief discussion, followed by a list of resources to help students grasp the appropriate concepts.

Assessment is not addressed in this book. Readers interested in this topic should consult the National Council of Teachers of Mathematics book *Assessment Standards for School Mathematics*, available for purchase from NCTM's offices at 1906 Association Drive, Reston, VA 22091-1593. It details the standards needed for an effective assessment system, the different purposes of assessment, and the issues, conditions, and challenges associated with changing to a new assessment system.

NOTES

1. *Curriculum and Evaluation Standards for School Mathematics* (Reston, Va.: National Council of Teachers of Mathematics, 1989) p. 16.

2. *Curriculum and Evaluation Standards for School Mathematics* (Reston, Va.: National Council of Teachers of Mathematics, 1989) pp. 17-19.

RESOURCES

Addresses of publishers or suppliers are listed in chapter 15.

Books

** Apelman, Maja, and Julie King. **Exploring Everyday Math: Ideas for Students, Teachers, and Parents**. Portsmouth, N.H.: Heinemann, 1993. 219p.

Atkinson, Sue, ed. **Mathematics with Reason**. Portsmouth, N.H.: Heinemann, 1992. 176p.

Baker, Ann, and Johnny Baker. **Mathematics in Process**. Portsmouth, N.H.: Heinemann, 1990. 170p.

McKeown, Ross. **Learning Mathematics: A Program for Classroom Teachers**. Portsmouth, N.H.: Heinemann, 1990. 139p.

Ohanian, Susan. **Garbage Pizza, Patchwork Quilts, and Math Magic**. New York: W. H. Freeman and Company, 1992. 256p.

Parker, Ruth E. **Mathematical Power: Lessons from a Classroom**. Portsmouth, N.H.: Heinemann, 1993. 229p.

** Schifter, Deborah, and Catherine Fosnot. **Reconstructing Mathematics Education**. New York: Teachers College Press, 1992. 256p. Available from Math Learning Center.

Stoessiger, Rex, and Joy Edmunds. **Natural Learning and Mathematics**. Portsmouth, N.H.: Heinemann, 1992. 113p.

Van de Walle, John A. **Elementary School Mathematics: Teaching Developmentally**. 2d ed. White Plains, N.Y.: Longman, 1994. 544p.

Whitin, David J., H. Mills, and T. O'Keefe. **Living and Learning Mathematics: Stories and Strategies for Supporting Mathematical Literacy**. Portsmouth, N.H.: Heinemann, 1991. 176p.

CHAPTER 1
MATHEMATICS AS PROBLEM SOLVING

In grades K-4, the study of mathematics should emphasize problem solving so that students can:

➤ use problem-solving approaches to investigate and understand mathematical content;

➤ formulate problems from everyday mathematical situations;

➤ develop and apply strategies to solve a wide variety of problems;

➤ verify and interpret results with respect to the original problem;

➤ acquire confidence in using mathematics meaningfully.

from *Curriculum and Evaluation Standards for School Mathematics*,
National Council of Teachers of Mathematics, 1989.

APPROACHES

One of the most fundamental skills that parents and teachers hope students acquire during their years of studying mathematics is the ability to solve problems. Although a number of these problems may be presented in lessons that come from books and work sheets, many problems will arise out of everyday situations. Those problems that arise "naturally" may even be the most effective teaching tool, because they help students discover a real purpose or application for the math they have studied.

There may be several different approaches to solving the same problem, and, for young children, many of these approaches involve manipulatives. Students should learn to value the solving of problems as well as the solution. Some approaches to problem solving will be faster than others. Some will involve paper and pencil, while other approaches may require manipulatives. One approach may be more appropriate in one setting than in another.

The curriculum should be rich in "real" problems that arise out of everyday home and school experiences. Such problems help students to make connections and to relate mathematics to their lives in meaningful ways. Opportunities will arise across the curriculum for students to use mathematics in solving problems in other content fields.

The resourceful parent who is not working with a standard curriculum can also supply problem-solving opportunities. By pointing out that, "Aunt Karen, Uncle Bob, and Tommy will be joining us for dinner tonight. Would you count out the silverware that we'll need and put it on the table?" a parent can pose a real problem for a young child.

When planning a trip, giving an older child a road map that shows the route to be traveled between two cities and asking that child to compute the number of miles between these two cities is another practical problem-solving opportunity that arises out of everyday experience.

Once a parent or teacher recognizes the richness of mathematical exploration in everyday contexts, more and more applications for solving problems will be found.

During these activities, students need the opportunity to interact with the teacher and other students to discuss the reasoning involved in the problem solving, to communicate how they decided to approach the problem, and to explain different approaches they might use. Allow time for students to identify and discuss possible connections they discovered.

RESOURCES

These resources may help teachers and parents to provide a rich mathematical environment for children. The titles under "Books" provide background reading and understanding. The books listed under "Other Resources" are primarily for student use and often contain reproducible pages. This section also lists games, manipulatives, videos, sets of materials, and computer programs. There are brief descriptions of each product. Although a supplier is listed, books may also be available directly from publishers, and books and other materials may be available from several distributors.

While efforts were made to be thorough, this resource list is not exhaustive. There are other companies that carry many fine products. In addition, new products are constantly coming on the market, and some of the items that are included may go out of print or be discontinued in the future.

This resource list, however, provides a range of available resources for teaching mathematics as problem solving.

Addresses of publishers or suppliers are listed in chapter 15.

Books

** Althouse, Rosemary. **Investigating Math with Young Children**. New York: Teachers College Press, 1994. 192p.
This book contains hands-on projects.

Baker, John, and Ann Baker. **From Puzzles to Projects: Solving Problems All the Way**. Portsmouth, N.H.: Heinemann, 1993. 138p.

Billstein, Rick. **A Problem Solving Approach to Mathematics for Elementary School Teachers**. Redwood City, Calif.: Benjamin/Cummings, 1990. 945p.

Brown, Stephen I., and Marion I. Walter, editors. **Problem Posing: Reflections and Applications**. Mahwah, N.J.: Lawrence Erlbaum Associates, 1993. 336p. All grades. Also available from Dale Seymour Publications.
This is a comprehensive collection of essays on the value of problem posing in math and other curricular areas.

** Burns, Marilyn. **Math for Smarty Pants**. Boston: Little, Brown, 1982. 128p.
Part 1 features Arithmetic with a Twist.

Dunn, Pat. **Math Trivial Pursuit, Intermediate**. Carthage, Ill.: Good Apple, 1991. 42p.
A Good Apple Math Activity Book for grades 4-6; it contains a game board and 232 question cards to reinforce basic math skills.

Erickson, Tim. **Get It Together: Math Problems for Groups**. Berkeley: University of California, Lawrence Hall of Science, 1989. 180p. Grades 4-12. Also available from Dale Seymour Publications.
This spiral-bound book uses clue cards to provide information to enable small groups to work together to solve problems.

Greenwood, Jay. **Developing Mathematical Thinking**. Portland, Oreg.: MESD Press, 1991. *Addition/Subtraction, Grades 1-4*, 356p. *Multiplication/Division, Grades 4-6*, 376p. Also available from Dale Seymour Publications.
Each book contains lessons, materials lists, assessment materials, and pedagogical discussion.

Kaye, Peggy. **Games for Math**. New York: Pantheon Books, 1988. 224p.
Strategy games are included.

Kelleher, Heather J. **Mathworks Book B**. Boston: Houghton Mifflin, 1992. 400p. Teacher's edition.
Problem solving is addressed under several of the topics and themes included.

Lenchner, George. **Mathematical Olympiad Contest Problems for Children**. East Meadow, N.Y.: Glenwood Publications, 1990. 176p. Grades 4-9. Also available from Dale Seymour Publications.
This is a collection of 250 problems from past years of Mathematical Olympiads with a four-step model for problem solving that includes hints, answers, and solution strategies.

Rowan, Thomas E., and Barbara Bourne. **Thinking Like Mathematicians: Putting the K-4 NCTM Standards into Practice**. Portsmouth, N.H.: Heinemann, 1994. 134p.

Skinner, Penny. **What's Your Problem? Posing and Solving Mathematical Problems, K-2**. Portsmouth, N.H.: Heinemann, 1991. 128p.

** Van de Walle, John A. **Elementary School Mathematics: Teaching Developmentally**. 2d ed. White Plains, N.Y.: Longman, 1994. 544p.
Chapter 4 discusses problem solving.

Other Resources
(manipulatives, games, sets, reproducibles, videos, and computer diskettes)

** **Attribute Blocks and Books**. Columbus, Ohio: Judy/Instructo.
Book 1 (Grades PreK-2) and *Book 2* (Grades 3-6) each contains 96 pages and challenges students to use problem solving and logical interpretation to complete activities. *Attribute Blocks* come in sets of 60 plastic blocks in five shapes, three colors, two sizes, and two thicknesses. Also available in a magnetic format and for overhead use.

Brainstorming: Activities for Creative Thinking. Worth, Ill.: Creative Publications.
By Craig Dickinson, Paula Dickinson, and Eileen Rideout. 144p. Grades 3-8.
This book contains strategies to teach brainstorming and divergent thinking, and more than 100 reproducible activity pages.

** **A Collection of Math Lessons**. Sausalito, Calif.: Math Solutions Publications. By M. Burns, B. Tank, and C. McLaughlin. Grades 1-8. Distributed by Cuisenaire Company of America.
This set of three books contains practical ideas for using problem solving to teach mathematics.

Cooperative Problem Solving. Worth, Ill.: Creative Publications. By Ann Roper. Grades 1-9.
Students are encouraged to share information, use math language, and discuss solution strategies. *Primary Cooperative Problem Solving Series*, Grades 1-3, contains four books using coins, pattern blocks, Linker Cubes, and Base Ten Blocks. A three-book series is available in Spanish. *Intermediate Cooperative Problem Solving Series*, Grades 3-6, is a six-book series using Base Ten Blocks, Attribute Blocks Fraction Pieces, Calculators, Tangrams, and Pattern Blocks. A three-book series is available in Spanish. *Cooperative Learning & Mathematics* by Beth Andrini, Grades K-8, is a 144-page resource book.

Domino Math. Worth, Ill.: Creative Publications. By Marcy Cook. 144p. Grades 3-6.
These reproducible lessons enhance problem-solving skills through the use of a single set of Double-Six Dominoes. *Double-Six Dominoes Set* is sold separately. Also available is a *Domino Math Starter Set* with the book and materials for four to six students and a *Double-Nine Dominoes Set*. *Overhead Double-Nine Dominoes* is also available.

** Hands-on Tangrams. Worth, Ill.: Creative Publications. 144p. Grades K-3.
Students' problem-solving skills are developed with tangram activities. The pages in the binder are reproducible. Also available are *Tangrams* in single sets, sets of 20, and sets of 30. *Hands-on Tangram Starter Set* contains binder and six sets of tangrams. *Hands-on Tangram Classroom Set* contains binder and 15 sets of tangrams. *Tangrams Sampler* contains the book, *Take Off with Tangrams*, and two buckets of tangrams. *Tangrams for the Overhead Projector* is also available.

** Linking Cubes. Columbus, Ohio: Judy/Instructo.
These 120 interlocking cubes in six colors provide hands-on experience in counting, comparing numbers, and problem solving. Cubes are 3/4 inch.

Magnetic Maze Game, Wooden. Boulder, Colo.: PlayFair Toys.
Children use magnetic wands to guide five metal balls through a maze to the center. Develops problem-solving skills and logical thinking. Game is fully enclosed so that parts can't be lost.

Make It Simpler. Reading, Mass.: Addison-Wesley. By Carol Meyer and Tom Sallee. 296p. Grades 4-8. Also available from Dale Seymour Publications.
These activities teach problem solving and include 100 reproducible problems.

 Math Blaster: In Search of Spot. Torrance, Calif.: Davidson and Associates. Computer diskette for DOS or Windows. Grades 1-6. Also available from NASCO.
Students help Blasternaut rescue his robot by solving problems. More than 500,000 problems available in addition, subtraction, multiplication, division, fractions, decimals, percents, estimation, and number patterns.

Math By-Lines. Palo Alto, Calif.: Dale Seymour Publications. By Carole Greenes, George Immerzeel, Linda Schulman, and Rika Spungin. 32p. Grades 3-4.
Students write word problems by filling in blanks within a story and then solve them. Has answers and blackline masters.

Math Contests. Palo Alto, Calif.: Dale Seymour Publications. By Steven R. Conrad and Daniel Fleger. Grades 4-8.
This is a set of three books with exciting challenges from national math competitions held between 1979 and 1991.

Math Cooperative Learning Activity Cards. Birmingham, Ala.: The Re-Print Corporation. Grades 2-6.
The set contains 128 cards that challenge students to apply math skills to real-life problem-solving situations.

Math Cross-Sections. Blacklick, Ohio: SRA/McGraw Hill. By Susan Ohanian. Grades 3-6.
This set contains posters, project cards, student reference books, and a teacher's guide to enable students to investigate intriguing, real-life topics and solve real-world problems.

Math Workshop. Novato, Calif.: Broderbund Software. Grades K-8. Also available from Egghead Software and others.
This computer game develops problem-solving skills and gives practice in basic computation. Available on CD.

Mathematics: Problem Solving Activities. Palo Alto, Calif.: Dale Seymour Publications. By D. Holmes, W. Klassen, and W. Szetela. Grades 3-6.

Each book of 80 pages contains reproducible problems that provide systematic approaches to problem solving, listing, patterning, sorting and classifying, guessing, and testing. Includes answers.

Mathematics for Teddy Bears: Problem Solving Activities for Young Children. Colchester, United Kingdom: Claire Publications. By Elizabeth Graham. 64p. Grades K-2. Also available from Dale Seymour Publications and others.

This book contains 30 illustrated activities to provide practice in counting, sorting, measuring, estimating, etc. Reproducible. Also available are *Three Bear Family Attribute Cards*, Grades K-3, which introduce students to attributes, sets, sequencing, and logic using double-sided cards and *Three Bear Family Counters* which are plastic bears in three sizes, three weights, and three colors in a set of 80.

Mathematics Games for Fun and Practice. Reading, Mass.: Addison-Wesley. By Alan Barson. Also available from Dale Seymour Publications.

Thirty-eight games help students develop problem-solving strategies and logical thinking.

 Mutanoid Math Challenge. Northridge, Calif.: Legacy Software. Computer diskette for IBM and compatibles. Grades 2-8. Available from NASCO.

This program contains outer space characters. Students engage in problem solving using operations, charts and graphs, and word problems.

Pentominoes. Palo Alto, Calif.: Dale Seymour Publications.

Each set contains 12, five-inch square pieces, each with a different shape. Also available are *Overhead Pentominoes*. *Pentomino Activities, Lessons, and Puzzles*, by Henri Picciotto, 288p., Grades 3-8, contains many reproducible pentomino exercises to practice measurement, strategic thinking, problem solving, etc. *Try It! Pentominoes*, by Marjorie Duby, Grades 4-9, is a set of original pentomino activities on challenge cards with a teacher's guide. *Problem Solving with Pentominoes*, by Alison Abrohms, 96p., Grades 1-4, is a collection of activities for individuals, small groups, and the whole class.

Poster: A Guide to Problem Solving. Palo Alto, Calif.: Dale Seymour Publications. Grades 4-12.

This 22-by-34-inch poster directs students through the problem-solving process.

Powerthink Books. Columbus, Ohio: Judy/Instructo. Available in *Levels 1, 2, 3, 4, 5, 6*.

Each book contains 64 pages and is designed to develop critical thinking and problem-solving skills in a cooperative learning setting. Books are reproducible.

The Problem Solver. Worth, Ill.: Creative Publications. By J. Goodnow, S. Hoogenboom, G. Moretti, M. Stephens, and A. Scanlin.

There is a problem-solving binder for each grade level, 1 through 8. Each binder contains 160 reproducible pages. *Grades 1* and *2* provide 54 lessons with 18 practice problems; *Grades 3* and *4* provide 48 lessons plus 72 practice problems. *Workbooks* are also available in sets of five. *The Problem Solver with Calculators for Grades 4-8* includes 20 teaching problems and is also available as a *Complete Set* with ten TI-108 calculators.

** **Problem Solving Activities with Unifix Cubes**. Rowley, Mass.: Didax Educational
Resources. By Janine Blinko and Noel Graham. 64p. Grades K-3.
These illustrated activities challenge students. Unifix cubes are required.

Problem Solving Experiences in Mathematics. Reading, Mass.: Addison Wesley
Longman, 1994. By Randall Charles, et al. Also available from Dale Seymour
Publications.
The set contains teacher sourcebooks and blackline masters. This program
(with one book for each grade level) helps students learn to approach problems
systematically and to recognize that there may be more than one strategy that can
be used with a problem.

Problem Solving Poster/Book Sets. Palo Alto, Calif.: Dale Seymour Publications.
Problem Parade, by Dale Seymour, Grades 4-6, contains posters and a 104-page
book. Students learn to recognize and work with patterns, number properties,
place value, logic, estimation, and visual perception. *Problem Play*, by Stephen
Currie, Grades 1-3, contains posters and an 88-page book. The set has 40
reproducible problems that require both logical and creative thinking.

The Puzzle File. Palo Alto, Calif.: Dale Seymour Publications. By James W. Perrin Jr.
These three reproducible books each provide more than 50 puzzles such as
codes, word scrambles, and mazes to give students creative problem-solving fun.
Included are *Back to School*, *Winter Wonderland*, and *Spring Fever*.

Solving Problems Kids Care About. Santa Monica, Calif.: Goodyear Publishing. By
Randall Souviney. Grades 4-8. Also available from Dale Seymour Publications.
This book contains 34 reproducible problems that help students understand
and design solution strategies.

Solving Story Problems: Problem-Solving Focus. Palo Alto, Calif.: Dale Seymour
Publications. By Carole Greenes, George Immerzeel, Linda Schulman, and
Rika Spungin. Grades 4-6.
This is a set of 100 cards containing multistep story problems at three levels
of difficulty. Comes with answers and suggestions for use.

Thinker Math, Grades 3-4. Worth, Ill.: Creative Publications. By Linda Schulman, Carole Greenes, and Rika Spungin.
This book has 96 pages and contains reproducible activities. It combines
critical thinking, analytical reading, and problem solving. Students read and
restore numbers so that the stories make sense.

Thinking Through Math Word Problems. Mahwah, N.J.: Lawrence Erlbaum
Associates, 1990. By Arthur Whimbey, Jack Lochhead, and Paula Potter. 147p.
Grades 4-6. Also available from Critical Thinking Press & Software.
Units include addition, subtraction, multiplication, division, and fractions.
The object of the book is to help students learn how to make word problems easier
to solve. Many of the problems were written by elementary school students. A
teacher's manual is available.

30 Wild and Wonderful Math Stories. New York: Scholastic. By Don Greenberg.
112p. Grades 4-8.
These reproducible stories teach basic skills such as multiplication, division,
fractions, percentages, and averages. Tips for students are provided.

TOPS Problem Solving Skill Sheets. Palo Alto, Calif.: Dale Seymour Publications. Grades 3-8.

This set consists of six books with 64 blackline masters each, along with answers to problems.

TOPS (Techniques of Problem Solving) PROGRAM. Palo Alto, Calif.: Dale Seymour Publications. Grades 3-8.

The complete *TOPS Beginning Problem Solving* (Grades K-2) contains four teacher resource books, one big book, and 350 durable plastic counting chips. Students learn to make drawings, find facts in pictures and tables, make tables, and use clues to solve problems. The books are sequenced moving from counting, to addition, to subtraction, to problems that require students to choose addition or subtraction. Also available are *TOPS Problem Solving Card Decks*, Grades 1-8. Each deck contains 200 illustrated problem-solving cards, with three levels of difficulty. Answer key and suggestions for use are included.

 Videokits. Pleasantville, N.Y.: Human Relations Media. Grades 4-8. Available from Silver Burdett Ginn.

This is a series of interactive problem-solving investigations designed to address the NCTM Standards. Each kit contains a teacher's resource book providing suggestions for using the videos, possible solution strategies, and blackline masters.

CHAPTER 2

MATHEMATICS AS COMMUNICATION

In grades K-4, the study of mathematics should include numerous opportunities for communication so that students can:

➤ relate physical materials, pictures, and diagrams to mathematical ideas;

➤ reflect on and clarify their thinking about mathematical ideas and situations;

➤ relate their everyday language to mathematical language and symbols;

➤ realize that representing, discussing, reading, writing, and listening to mathematics are a vital part of learning and using mathematics.

from *Curriculum and Evaluation Standards for School Mathematics*,
National Council of Teachers of Mathematics, 1989.

APPROACHES

Students learn their native language through verbal communication. They also need to learn the language of mathematics as well as its symbols and representations of mathematical ideas. Once they understand, for example, what an equation is, they can see its utility in representing a variety of problems.

When a young student is working on a problem, a teacher or other adult should frequently ask that child to talk aloud, which helps the adult follow the child's reasoning process and helps increase the child's understanding and clarify his or her thinking. Students may use pictures or objects to represent their reasoning process.

Sometimes students may also be encouraged to write an explanation of a math project in which they have been involved. This cross-curricular blend of writing and mathematics is an important means of clarifying thinking and of building a math vocabulary. Mathematical language appropriately enters the language-arts journal and the science-lab book.

Some of the sources listed include cooperative learning techniques with which students work together in small groups. Such group efforts demand clear communication and careful listening to others' explanations and ideas.

Many books are being written for students in kindergarten through fourth grades that deliberately or incidentally include mathematics. Some encourage counting, problem solving, or the use of shapes or concepts in interesting ways. Such books provide valuable links in connecting mathematics to the total curriculum as a part of meaningful learning.

RESOURCES

These resources may help teachers and parents provide a rich mathematical environment for children. The titles under "Books" provide background reading and understanding. The books listed under "Other Resources" are primarily for student use and often contain reproducible pages. This section also includes games, manipulatives, videos, sets of materials, computer programs and brief descriptions of each product. Although a supplier is listed, books may also be available directly from publishers, and books and other materials may be available from several distributors.

Although efforts were made to be thorough, this resource list is not exhaustive. There are other companies that carry many fine products. In addition, new products are constantly coming on the market, and some of the items that are included may go out of print or be discontinued in the future.

This resource list, however, provides a range of available resources for teaching mathematics as communication.

Addresses of publishers and suppliers are listed in chapter 15.

Books

Bickmore-Brand, Jennie, ed. **Language in Mathematics**. Portsmouth, N.H.: Heinemann, 1993. 116p.

** Burns, Marilyn. "Having a Mathematical Conversation." Part 3 of **Math for Smarty Pants**. Boston: Little, Brown, 1982. 128p.

Cutting, Brian, and Jillian Cutting. **Captain B's Boat**. Bothell, Wash.: The Wright Group, 1988. 16p.

——. **Math Is Everywhere**. Bothell, Wash.: The Wright Group, 1988. 16p.

——. **Sunshine Street**. Bothell, Wash.: The Wright Group, 1988. 16p.

Greenes, Carole, George Immerzeel, Linda Schulman, and Rika Spungin. **Math Predictable Storybooks**. Blacklick, Ohio: SRA/McGraw Hill, 1989.
Titles in the set include *Opossum in a Tree*; *Which Hare Is Where?*; *The Magic Shapes*; *Rebecca's Party*; *Jake's Closet*; *I Can, You Can*. A teacher's guide and blackline masters are also included.

** Lilburn, Pat, and Pam Rawson. **Let's Talk Math**. Portsmouth, N.H.: Heinemann, 1994. 106p. Also available from Institute for Math Mania.

This book shows primary teachers how everyday language can be used effectively in describing mathematical experiences.

Teaching Committee, The Mathematical Association. **Math Talk**. Portsmouth, N.H.: Heinemann, 1990. 66p.

** Whitin, David J., H. Mills, and T. O'Keefe. **Living and Learning Mathematics: Stories and Strategies for Supporting Mathematical Literacy**. Portsmouth, N.H.: Heinemann, 1991. 176p.

Students discover math as they look around their environment.

Other Resources

(manipulatives, games, sets, reproducibles, videos, and computer diskettes)

** **Addition Stories**. Crystal Lake, Ill.: Rigby.

These stories explore the concept of addition. Each title is available as a big book, a set of six small books, and a cassette. Titles that focus on using numbers up to ten are *Birds, Birds, Everywhere; What's in the Cupboard?; Penny Penguin's Party; Fish for Supper*. These addition stories focus on numbers through 22: *Shiny Shells, Addtron, Sad King Cole, A Strange Stew*.

Book into Math. Lincolnshire, Ill.: Learning Resources. By Laureen Walton, Gayle White, and Debbie Wigley. 144p. Grades K-3. Available from ETA.

This resource book encourages reading and discussing a story in class. Popular children's stories and classics are included.

Books You Can Count on Linking Mathematics and Literature. Portsmouth, N.H.: Heinemann, 1991. By Rachel Griffiths and Margaret Clyne. 112p. Grades K-3.

This resource contains 40 lessons based on stories and poems that tie math into other curricular areas.

 Counting on Frank: Math Adventures. San Mateo, Calif.: Creative Wonders/Electronic Arts. Also available from Egghead Software.

This computer game is available on CD and allows students to apply math concepts to the world around them.

** **Equal Group Stories**. Crystal Lake, Ill.: Rigby.

The stories introduce students to the concept of equal groups. Each title is available as a big book, a set of six small books, and a cassette. The titles include *Frog on a Log, Mirror Mirror, Shoe's in Twos*, and *Zany Zoo*. Titles that extend the division concept and involve students in problem-solving situations include *Peter Piper, Tap and Rap, Mr. McMunch*, and *The Great Carrot Mystery*.

** = **Highly recommended.**   = **Computer resources.**   = **Videos.**

Fizz and Martina Primary Video Kits. Watertown, Mass.: Tom Snyder Productions. Grades K-3. Also available from Creative Publications.

Each of the three titles in the series provides students with practice in speaking and writing the language of math: *Buddies for Life*, *The Caves of Blue Falls*, and *The Fantastic Fall Fair*. Each kit includes student workbooks, a teacher's guide, cards, blackline masters, and an illustrated big book.

 Kingdom of Wisdom. Vernon Hills, Ill.: ETA. Grades 3-7.

The set contains a video, eight student storybooks, a teacher's guide, a reproducible game board, and playing pieces. Students complete the video story by working cooperatively to solve math problems.

Krypto. Grades 4-10. Available from several distributors, including Dale Seymour Publications.

In this game, which includes 52 cards, a game book, and a score pad, players combine numbers by addition, subtraction, multiplication, and division to reach a given number within 30 seconds.

Math Mats: Hands-on Activities for Young Children. Blacklick, Ohio: SRA/McGraw Hill. By Carol Thornton and Judith Wells.

Set 1's themes for kindergarten are *My School Day*, *A Hike in the Forest*, *Bear's Birthday Party*, and *Dinosaur Land*. Set 2's themes for Grade 1 are *Let's Go Shopping*, *Let's Go for a Ride*, *At the Amusement Park*, and *Fun in the Circus*. Sets of colorful mats and punch-out animal counters are used to teach classification, patterning, prenumber readiness, counting, numbers, addition, and subtraction.

Math Talk. Portsmouth, N.H.: Heinemann, 1990. By Mathematical Association Staff. 66p. Also available from ETA.

This short book demonstrates the importance of spoken language in the mastery of mathematics.

Raps and Rhymes in Maths. Portsmouth, N.H.: Heinemann, 1991. By Ann Baker and Johnny Baker. 96p. Grades K-4. Also available from ETA.

This collection of rhymes, riddles, and stories has a mathematics theme and includes activities that suggest possible math investigations.

** **Sharing Number Stories**. Crystal Lake, Ill.: Rigby.

Each title is available as a big book, a set of six small books, and a cassette. The following stories focus on sharing things that number less than ten: *The Bears' Berries*, *Even Steven*, *The Nice Mice*, and *The Pixies' Toyshop*. These stories help show multiplication as equal groups: *The Red Shed*, *A Dozen Dizzy Dinosaurs*, *The Pirate's Gold*, and *Goats in Boats*.

Storytime, Mathtime: Discovering Math in Children's Literature. Palo Alto, Calif.: Dale Seymour Publications. By Patricia Satariano. Grades 1-3.

This teacher book has math lessons derived from 18 children's books. The books are also available from this supplier. Titles include *A Chair for My Mother*; *Caps for Sale*; *Cherries and Cherry Pits*; *Cloudy with a Chance of Meatballs*; *Corduroy*; *Curious George Rides a Bike*; *Each Orange Had 8 Slices*; *Frog and Toad Are Friends*; *Geraldine's Blanket*; *Grandfather Tang's Story*; *How Big Is a Foot?*; *How Many Snails?*; *Knots on a Counting Rope*; *Millions of Cats*; *Mouse Count*; *Mr. Grumpy's Outing*; *Nine O'Clock Lullaby*; *Senefer, A Young Genius in Old Egypt*; *Something Special for Me*; *Strega Nona*; *The Doorbell Rang*; *The Grouchy Ladybug*; *The Relatives Came*; *Two Ways to Count to Ten*; and *Who Sank the Boat?*

Subtraction Stories. Crystal Lake, Ill.: Rigby.

These stories explore the "take away" aspect of subtraction. Each title is available as a big book, a set of six small books, and a cassette. These titles use numbers under ten: *Ten Silly Sheep, The Wizard's Wand, The Mean Machine*, and *The Queen of Hearts*. These stories introduce students to the missing addend concept: *Paint a Rainbow, Hurry Hurry, The Lazy Shepherd*, and *Our Sister's Surprise*.

** **TOPS Communication Card Decks**. Palo Alto, Calif.: Dale Seymour Publications. By Carole Greenes, Linda Schulman, and Rika Spungin. Grades 1-6.

There are three decks of cards. Each contains 200 cards that have been color coded according to their difficulty and that can be used with individuals or groups. The problems challenge students to explain their thinking steps, justify their solutions, describe patterns, find alternative solutions, and make predictions.

20 Thinking Questions for Rainbow Centimeter Cubes. Worth, Ill.: Creative Publications. 112p. Grades 3-6.

Students are asked to solve these 20 problems and then communicate their thinking through discussion and writing. *Rainbow Centimeter Cubes* are sold separately and packaged in sets of 1,000 cubes. The book and cubes are also sold as *Starter Sets* for eight students and as *Classroom Kits* for 32 students working in pairs. Also available are *Geometry Jobcards: Cubes* for Grades 5-8.

24 Game. Grade 4 and up. Available from several distributors, including Dale Seymour Publications.

The 96 double-sided cards are arranged in three levels of difficulty and offer 192 challenges. The tournament kit contains a poster, certificates, and other items to support a tournament. Students use all the numbers on a card and any combination of addition, subtraction, multiplication, and division to get 24. It comes in addition, subtraction, multiplication, division, and fraction editions as well as in a complete set.

Wallhangings. Richardson, Tex.: Kaidy Educational Resources. PreK and up.

These felt wall hangings come in a variety of sizes and include backgrounds, felt objects, numbers, and operational signs. Available are: *Supermarket Learn to Count, Perpetual Calendar, Time Clock, Learn to Count, Soft Learn to Count Blocks, Number Fun*, and *Counting Stories*.

WorkMat Math: Getting Started. Worth, Ill.: Creative Publications. By Micaellia Randolph Brummett and Linda Holden. Grades K-1.

Storyboard activities give young students an introduction to the language of math. Words such as *all, some, more than, first*, and *beside* are included in the vocabulary. A teacher's guide explains 12 lessons. Sets include counters in appropriate shapes. Available are *Puddleduck Lake, Billygoat Barnyard*, and *Bustle-town Square*. These can also be purchased as a series.

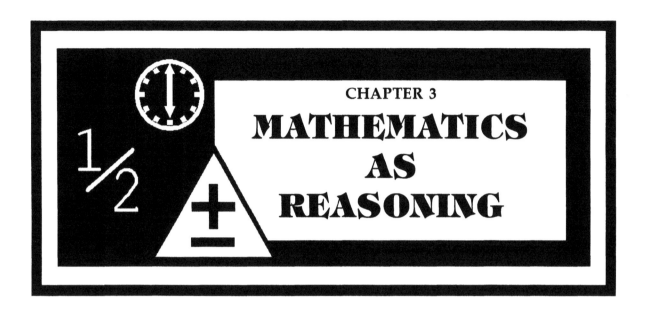

CHAPTER 3

MATHEMATICS AS REASONING

In grades K-4, the study of mathematics should emphasize reasoning so that students can:

- draw logical conclusions about mathematics;
- use models, known facts, properties, and relationships to explain their thinking;
- justify their answers and solution processes;
- use patterns and relationships to analyze mathematical situations;
- believe that mathematics makes sense.

from *Curriculum and Evaluation Standards for School Mathematics*,
National Council of Teachers of Mathematics, 1989.

APPROACHES

This standard was not proposed as a means of introducing formal reasoning into the early-elementary-school curriculum. But mathematics is reasoning, and students should learn to apply critical thinking to their problem solving.

Teachers and parents can help foster a spirit of inquiry by asking such questions as, Why do you think that's a good answer? How did you come to that conclusion? What steps did you take in thinking this through? Can you explain what ideas you had but discarded as you worked to come up with that answer?

When a student has solved a problem, the child needs an opportunity to explain or justify the solution. Perhaps the student wants to use objects in explanation or wants to draw a representation. Whatever the means, the explanation may solidify the student's thinking or suggest an error in that thinking. It's a valuable discussion process regardless of whether the student is talking with an adult or another student.

Peers can be a great help in clarifying thinking. It's always interesting to watch a group of students share the ways in which they solved a problem. The discussion may reveal that a single problem may be approached in several ways, many of which would be successful.

Critical-thinking skills are certainly not confined to the discipline of mathematics. Students use these same problem-solving skills across the curriculum: in science, social studies, and the arts.

These thinking activities are part of a process in which mathematical reasoning develops. Students need many opportunities to think through and create as well as to solve problems.

RESOURCES

These resources may help teachers and parents provide a rich mathematical environment for children. The titles under "Books" provide background reading and understanding. Those listed under "Other Resources" are primarily for student use and often contain reproducible pages. This section also includes games, manipulatives, videos, sets of materials, and computer programs. There are brief descriptions of each product. Although a supplier is listed, books may also be available directly from publishers, and books and other materials may be available from several distributors.

Although attempts were made to be thorough, this resource list is not exhaustive. There are other companies that carry many fine products. In addition, new products are constantly coming on the market, and some of the items that are included may go out of print or be discontinued in the future.

This resource list, however, provides a range of available resources for teaching mathematics as reasoning.

Addresses of publishers and suppliers are listed in chapter 15.

Books

Brown, Sam. **Instant Math**. Nashville, Tenn.: Incentive Publications, 1991. 144p. Grades K-3.

This book includes suggestions for finding simple manipulatives in the home and classroom.

** Burns, Marilyn. "Logical Puzzles." Part 4 in **Math for Smarty Pants**. Boston: Little, Brown, 1982. 128p.

This book contains intriguing puzzles.

Kaye, Peggy. **Games for Math**. New York: Pantheon Books, 1987. 236p.

This book includes a variety of strategy games and number puzzles.

Kelleher, Heather J. **Mathworks Book B**. Boston: Houghton Mifflin, 1992. 400p.

This book contains sections on patterns and strategy.

** Rasmussen, Greta. **Brain Stations**. Stanwood, Wash.: Tin Man Press, 1989. 112p. Grades 2-6. Also available from Dale Seymour Publications.

Included are 50 activity suggestions for students working at learning stations. Includes illustrated directions.

** Suid, Murray, and Wanda Lincoln. **Ten-Minute Thinking Tie-Ins**. Palo Alto, Calif.: Dale Seymour Publications, 1992. 128p. Grades 2-6.

This book offers a variety of activities for practice in fundamental thinking, brainstorming, categorizing, hypothesizing, analyzing, and visualizing.

Other Resources

(manipulatives, games, sets, reproducibles, videos, and computer diskettes)

Abalone Game. Worth, Ill.: Creative Publications. Grade 4-adult.

This board and marble game has a wide range of possible moves.

AlphaShapes. Palo Alto, Calif.: Dale Seymour Publications.

The 52-piece set includes 26 pairs of polygons in green and orange and an instruction book.

** **Attribute Blocks**. Worth, Ill.: Creative Publications. Grades K-9.

A set contains 60 blocks in five shapes, three colors, two sizes, and two thicknesses. Available in three sizes are *Pocket Attribute Blocks*, *Desk-Top Attribute Blocks*, and *Group Attribute Blocks*. Also available are *Attribute Blocks for the Overhead Projector* and *Classic Graphing Mat*. *Hands-on Attribute Blocks Binder*, 144p., encourages students to investigate and contains many reproducible pages. The set also comes as *Hands-on Attribute Blocks Starter Set* and includes a binder and materials for four to six students. *Moving on with Attribute Blocks*, by Judy Goodnow, Grades 4-6, 128p., provides for problem-solving experiences and includes many reproducibles; *Moving on with Attribute Blocks Starter Set* includes the binder and materials for four to six students. *Cooperative Problem Solving with Attribute Blocks*, by Judy Goodnow, Grades 4-6, provides 80 thought-provoking logic problems and is also sold as a *Class Set* with *Pocket Attribute Blocks*.

** **Attribute Blocks**. Palo Alto, Calif.: Dale Seymour Publications.

These are available in sets of various sizes. *Attribute Logic Blocks* come in a set of 60 plastic blocks in three colors, two sizes, and two thicknesses. These are also available as *Attribute Logic Blocks for the Overhead Projector*. *ESS Attribute Blocks* are available in a set of 32 plastic blocks in four colors and two sizes. Also available is the book *Exploring Attributes*, by Maria Marolda, Grades 1-8, which contains blackline masters and features four types of activities, including teaching notes, discussion questions, and extension activities.

** **Attribute Blocks**. Rowley, Mass.: Didax Educational Resources.

These blocks are available as a *Class Set*, a *Group Set*, a *Desk Set*, and a *Pocket Set*. There are 60 shapes, each made of heavy plastic. Each set comes with a *Learning by Logic* booklet. Also available is an *Attribute Logic Book*, which contains 32 pages of suggested activities for problem solving, logical interpretations, and demonstrating mathematical concepts.

** = **Highly recommended.**   = **Computer resources.**   ▦ = **Videos.**

** **Attribute Blocks**. Birmingham, Ala.: The Re-Print Corporation. Grades K-6.

These 60-piece sets come in a variety of sizes, including *Giant Attribute Blocks, Attribute Block Pocket Set, Attribute Block Desk Set,* and *Overhead Attribute Blocks.* Also available are *Attribute Logic Book,* which includes instructions for use of the blocks; *Attribute Block Activity Cards,* which has a teacher's guide; and *Attribute Block Template.*

Attribute Desk Blocks. Columbus, Ohio: Judy/Instructo.

In using the 60-piece set, students apply sorting, classification, matching, and logic-building skills. The set contains five shapes, three colors, two sizes, and two thicknesses.

Attribute Sorting Set. Birmingham, Ala.: The Re-Print Corporation. Grades K-1.

This set contains more than 200 beads, pegs, blocks, and discs of different textures plus an 11-compartment plastic storage tray and detailed activity booklet.

Building Thinking Skills. Palo Alto, Calif.: Dale Seymour Publications. Grades K-10.

Primary (Grades K-2) and *Book 1 (Grades 2-4)* come with a teacher's and a student's edition. Lesson plans, teaching suggestions, answers, and blackline masters are included. Each contains activities to develop skills in identifying similarities and sometimes differences, in recognizing and completing sequences, and in determining classification and drawing analogies.

** **Challenge Magazine**. Palo Alto, Calif.: Dale Seymour Publications. By Carole Greenes, George Immerzeel, Linda Schulman, and Rika Spungin. 128p. Grades 4-6.

Eight, 16-page reproducible magazines allow students to solve cases and puzzles. Teaching notes and answers are included.

Colored Cubes and Books. Rowley, Mass.: Didax Educational Resources.

These books present patterns of cubes seen from above or from an angle. Students arrange cubes to reproduce the pattern. Set includes 30 cubes and three pattern books.

Critical Thinking Activities. Palo Alto, Calif.: Dale Seymour Publications. By Dale Seymour and Ed Beardslee. Grades K-12.

A set of three activity booklets helps students develop important elements of critical thinking, including studying pattern activities, developing imagery activities, and solving logic problems. Blackline masters and answer keys included.

** **Critical Thinking Activities for Mathematics**. Pacific Grove, Calif.: Critical Thinking Press & Software. By Anita Harnadek. *Book 1,* Grades 2-4.

Problems are presented that require reasoning and critical thinking. Many reproducibles are included, and a teacher's guide is available.

Discover! Palo Alto, Calif.: Dale Seymour Publications. Grades 2-6.

Each deck focuses on an ordinary object, such as a pencil, button, or hand. There are 12 decks of 20 activity cards per set. Each set has questions and projects that encourage students to explore different aspects of an object.

Games Magazine Junior Kids' Big Book of Games. Palo Alto, Calif.: Dale Seymour Publications. Karen C. Anderson, editor. Grade 3 and up.

This is a collection of 140 games, including logic puzzles.

Got It! Rowley, Mass.: Didax Educational Resources.

In this challenging card game, visual patterns are formed when a dealer lays laminated, patterned cards in a sequence. Players must figure out the pattern rule and explain how they discovered it. Instructions are included.

Group Solutions. Berkeley, Calif.: University of California, Lawrence Hall of Science, 1992. By Jan M. Goodman. 144p. Also available from Dale Seymour Publications.

Activity suggestions for groups of four promote cooperative, logical thinking. Uses maps, science, and mapping skills.

 ** Hands-on Equations. Allentown, Pa.: Borenson & Associates, 1994. By Henry Borenson. Grades 3-4.

The kit introduces algebra to third and fourth graders and includes manipulatives, a video, and manuals.

Logic Connections. Palo Alto, Calif.: Dale Seymour Publications. By Judy Bippert and Jeannette Steiger. 152p. Grades 3-4.

By using such aids as manipulatives and writing, these guided activities simulate real-life situations. Includes blackline masters for each activity.

Logic Problems for Primary People. Worth, Ill.: Creative Publications. By Valerie Stofac and Anne Wesley. 144p. Grades 1-3.

This illustrated book's jungle adventures challenge students to use patterns and analyze data. Contains reproducible pages.

Logic Sheets/Venn Diagrams. Rowley, Mass.: Didax Educational Resources.

These large 29½-inch-by-20-inch work mats are printed on both sides and illustrate two separate circles, a two-way Venn diagram, a three-way Venn diagram, and a seven-by-seven-square matrix.

LogicTalk Poster Puzzles. Worth, Ill.: Creative Publications. By Honi Bamberger, Josepha Robles, and Brenda Hammond. Grades K-2.

These theme-based posters help in building logic skills through oral-language activities. Each set comes with an 80-page teacher's guide and three 19-inch-by-24½-inch posters. There are 24 logic problems for each poster. A *LogicTalk Poster Puzzles Complete Set* is available along with individual titles, including *Back-to-School, Winter, Spring, Animal Friends, Coins and Clocks,* and *Holidays.*

Mancala. Worth, Ill.: Creative Publications. Grade 1-adult.

This logic game is played with a board and balls and includes instructions.

Manipulative Activities to Build Algebraic Thinking. Pacific Grove, Calif.: Critical Thinking Press & Software. By Bob Willcutt. Grades 4-9.

This set of three books helps students make a transition between concrete and abstract reasoning in mathematics. *Book A1* uses single types of manipulatives, such as tiles. *Book B1* requires manipulatives that can be used to represent place value, such as Cuisenaire rods. *Book C1* uses manipulatives of multiple colors and shapes, such as pattern blocks.

Mastermind. Grade 3 and up. Available from most distributors, including Dale Seymour Publications.

This is a class game of logic and strategy.

Masterminds Riddle Math Series. Nashville, Tenn.: Incentive Publications. Grade 3 and up.

This is a set of five books, each of which contains 96 pages. The titles in the set include *Decimals, Percentages, Metric System, and Consumer Math; Fractions, Ratio, Probability, and Standard Measurement; Addition, Subtraction, Place Value, and Other Numeration Systems; Multiplication and Division,* all by Brenda Opie, Lory Jackson, and Douglas McAvinn; and *Geometry and Graphing,* by Brenda Opie, Lory Jackson, Douglas McAvinn, and Nancy Ygnve.

 ** Math Blaster: Secret of the Lost City. Torrance, Calif.: Davidson and Associates. Grades 3-6. Also available from Egghead Software.

This computer game gives students practice in logical thinking, percentages, and applying concepts to shapes and objects. Available on CD and 3½-inch disks.

** Math Discoveries with Attribute Blocks. Montpelier, Vt.: Institute for Math Mania. By Judy Goodnow. 64p. Grades 1-3.

Students gain practice in recognizing similarities and differences using attribute blocks. Contains 40 reproducible activities.

 Math Mind Benders. Pacific Grove, Calif.: Critical Thinking Press & Software. By Anita Harnadek.

The five-book series presents activities that use inductive and deductive reasoning, with the challenge to the student's reasoning skills increasing at each level. Each 28-page book includes many reproducible activities. The series is also available as *Math Mind Benders Software,* program by Eric Thornton, for use on Apple, IBM, and Macintosh systems.

 Math Mystery Theatre. Birmingham, Ala.: The Re-Print Corporation. Grades 2-8.

These 40-minute videos come with blackline masters and a teacher's guide and present various math concepts in a mystery-story setting. They are available as individual videos, as sets of six, or in a complete set of 24 videos. Titles include *Case of the Stolen Sums; Subtraction Roundup; Multiplication Maniac; Mission Division: Case of the Dazzling Diamonds; Mission Division: World's Secret Formula; Great Numbers Bank Robbery; Multiple Adventures of Math Man; Fraction Freaks; Strange Case of the Fractured Fresco; Fractionstein; Fraction Action; Case of the Kidnapped Kid; Decimal Disaster or the Case of the Maltese Fraction; Decimal Disagreement: The War of the Rose; Case of the Unfinished Orchestra; Kong Fu: The 100% Solution; The Metric Meddler; Curse of the Tomb of King Tut Tut Cubit; The Thick Man; Gang with a Difference; The "Pie Is Square" Case; Mathman and Chickadee vs. the Questioner; Tarzap and the Case of the Disappearing Jungle;* and *The Ten Percenters.*

Mathematical Reasoning Through Verbal Analysis. Pacific Grove, Calif.: Critical Thinking Press & Software. By Warren Hill and Ronald Edwards. *Book 1,* 188p., Grades 2-4; *Book 2,* 288p., Grades 4-8.

These books use fundamental operations and mathematical skills to teach students to reason mathematically. A teacher's manual is available for each book.

Mosaic Magic. Mahwah, N.J.: Troll Learn & Play.

Students make colorful patterns by moving beads into slots. They can match pattern cards or create their own designs. The set comes with a carrying case and 150 marbles.

Multilink Cubes and Prisms. Glen Burnie, Md.: NES Arnold. Grades K-6. Also available from Dale Seymour Publications.

These come in sets of cubes and prisms and in transparent squares. The cubes connect on all six sides. The prisms are equilateral triangles and connect to the cubes. *Multilink Isos Task Cards*, Grade 2 and up, are a set of ten cards for use with *Multilink Isos Triangular Prisms* and other Multilink shapes. *Multilink Isos Triangular Prisms*, Grade 2 and up, are right-angled isosceles triangles with two-centimeter sides and are compatible with Multilink cubes and prisms. *Multilink Explorations*, by P. McLean, M. Laycock, and L. Hovis, Grades 1-6, is a 48-page book of work sheets, including teacher notes. *Multilink Activity Cards*, by R. J. Stone, Grades K-6, is a set of 40 cards that provides for exploration of three-dimensional construction.

** **Numbers and Patterns Math Kit**. Columbus, Ohio: Judy/Instructo.

Includes 102 rainbow math cubes, 500 rainbow links, 300 counters, 250 plastic pattern blocks, storage buckets, and a container.

** **100 Activities for the Hundred Number Board**. Worth, Ill.: Creative Publications. By Sandra Pryor Clarkson. 80p. Grades 1-8.

These reproducible activities explore many math concepts, including identifying number patterns. Also available is a *Hundred Wall Chart*. The *Hundred Number Board Complete Classroom Kit* contains the activities book, 60 laminated hundred number boards, one hundred number board and tiles, one overhead hundred number board, a wall chart with numeral cards, and two buckets of color tiles. The *Hundred Number Tiles*, *Overhead Hundred Number Tiles*, *Overhead Hundred Number Boards Set*, *Hundred Number Board and Tiles*, *Laminated Hundred Number Boards*, and *Overhead Hundred Number Boards Deluxe Set* are available separately.

Parquetry Blocks, **Parquetry Patterns**, and **Desk Top Parquetry Blocks Set**. Columbus, Ohio: Judy/Instructo.

The desktop sets include eight ten-by-ten-inch pattern cards, 32 wooden blocks in three shapes and six colors, and a 12-inch-by-12-inch inlay tray. The parquetry blocks are available in desktop or jumbo size and include 32 wooden blocks in three shapes and six colors plus a teaching guide. The parquetry patterns include 12 pattern cards and a teaching guide.

** **Pattern Block Sets**. Palo Alto, Calif.: Dale Seymour Publications.

These are available in a variety of sets. *Price Buster Pattern Blocks*, Grades K-9, are available in 250-piece sets of plastic in multiple colors. *Pattern Blocks* are available in wood or plastic and include a set of four mirrors. *Pattern Blocks for Overhead Projection* consists of 49 transparent colored blocks. *Pattern Block Template* is a tool for tracing the six basic pattern-block shapes and creating activities. *Pattern Block Activities*, by Barbara Bayha and Katy Burt, Grades K-8, is an 80-page reproducible book that encourages exploration with pattern-block activities. Task cards are available separately.

** **Pattern Block Sets**. Columbus, Ohio: Judy/Instructo.

These sets are available in *Beginning Pattern Blocks Activity Cards*, Grades PreK-1, and *Symmetrical Designs Using Pattern Blocks*, Grades 2-4. Sets include task cards, activity cards, teaching guides, and 250 plastic pattern blocks. The items may be purchased in sets, or cards and blocks may be purchased separately. Transparent pattern blocks are also available for overhead use.

Pattern Link Set. Columbus, Ohio: Judy/Instructo. Grades PreK-1.

This set has more than 35 activities for exploring variations of patterns and includes 500 Rainbow Links and self-correcting task cards with two levels of problems. *Rainbow Links* can be purchased separately in sets of 500 plastic links in six bright colors in a storage bucket. *Deluxe Links Sets* are available that include Rainbow Links and Pattern Cards as well as a set of *Count & Compare Activities Cards*. Also available is an *Overhead Rainbow Links* set for demonstration.

Pattern Recognition, Sorting and Grouping Material. Rowley, Mass.: Didax Educational Resources.

The set contains five boxes of materials. Each box contains six one-inch plastic design cubes and three 3½-inch-by-seven-inch two-sided laminated cards. Students match the design on the cube to the design on the card. Instructions are included.

Playing with Logic, Discover Logic, Adventures with Logic. Columbus, Ohio: Fearon Teacher Aids, 1985. By Mark Schoenfield and Jeannette Rosenblatt. 64p. each. Grades 3-7. Also available from Dale Seymour Publications.

These games and puzzles provides practice with classification, sequencing, inference, deduction, and creative logic. Answers and teacher's guides are included.

Poster: Who Did It? By Adam Case. Grade 3 and up. Available from Dale Seymour Publications.

The poster describes different scenarios to figure out who did it and who didn't do it.

Prolific Thinkers' Guide. Palo Alto, Calif.: Dale Seymour Publications. By Gary Carnow and Constance Gibson. 96p. Grades 3-8.

This material helps students in generating solutions, brainstorming, categorizing, and flow charting in preparation for "The Prolific Thinkers' Marathon," in which they compete as teams to solve problems. Includes reproducible forms.

Puzzle Tables. By Thomas C. O'Brien. 64p. Grades 4-8. Available from Dale Seymour Publications.

To complete these reproducible puzzle tables students must search for number patterns and understand how numbers are combined. Answers and a teacher's guide are included.

Rainbow Bead Pattern Cards. Columbus, Ohio: Judy/Instructo.

Patterns begin with one shape and one color and progress to four shapes and six colors. There are 52 activities and 20 task cards. These cards are designed to be used with Rainbow Beads, which come in ¾-inch and ½-inch sizes. These sets contain laces as well as wooden beads in six colors and four shapes.

Rainbow Math Cubes and **Rainbow Math Cube Pattern Cards**. Columbus, Ohio: Judy/Instructo.

Twenty self-correcting task cards feature more than 75 activities. With four levels of problem-solving activities, students discover patterns and three-dimensional constructions that develop logical thinking skills. The math cubes are in sets of 102 cubes in six bright colors and are packed in a storage bucket.

Scratch Your Brain Where It Itches: Math Games, Tricks, and Quick Activities.
Pacific Grove, Calif.: Critical Thinking Press & Software. By Doug Brumbaugh
and Linda Brumbaugh. *Book A-1*, Grades 1-3; and *Book B-1*, Grades 3-6.
These books contain activities that motivate students to solve problems by
engaging critical- and creative-thinking skills. Both books contain more than 40
reproducible pages.

Sorting Toys. Worth, Ill.: Creative Publications. Grades K-2.
The set, which is packed in a bucket, contains 160 plastic toys for such
activities as sorting, counting, and identifying attributes. Includes animals, fruits,
vegetables, cars, boats, and planes.

** **Thinker Games**. Worth, Ill.: Creative Publications. By Linda Holden and Ann
Roper. 144p.
The set is filled with 120 games that provide practice in three types of logical
thinking. Most games are for two players, and the pages are reproducible. *Thinker
Tasks: Critical Thinking Activities*, by Linda Holden, 144p., Grades 4-6, contains
three sections: Attributes and Logic, Number Patterns, and Visual Perception.
Available game supplies include spinners, dice, operations dice, wooden cubes,
overhead dot dice, spinners, and templates for the overhead.

The Thinker's Toolbox. Palo Alto, Calif.: Dale Seymour Publications. By Pamela
Thornburg and David Thornburg. 144p. Grades 3-8.
This book introduces key words and techniques and offers challenging
problems. Includes teacher's notes and reproducible handouts.

Thinking Connections: Learning to Think and Thinking to Learn. Reading, Mass.:
Addison Wesley Longman, 1993. By D. Perkins, H. Goodrich, J. Owen, and
S. Tishman. 144p. Grades 4-8. Also available from Dale Seymour Publications.
Students learn to organize and evaluate thinking and use a three-step process
for decision making. Includes wall posters, assessment material, and suggestions
for infusing thinking strategies into the classroom.

Triango! Worth, Ill.: Creative Publications. Grade 3-adult.
This game of logic and strategic thinking uses a triangular game board. The
Teacher's Guide, by Behrouz Aghevli and Mark A. Spikell, is available separately.

Try-a-Tile: Logic with Numbers. Worth, Ill.: Creative Publications. By Marcy
Cook. Grades 4-6.
This material contains 40 two-sided activity cards and involves deductive
and inductive reasoning. Numeral Tiles are necessary for the activity but are
sold separately.

CHAPTER 4

MATHEMATICAL CONNECTIONS

In grades K-4, the study of mathematics should include opportunities to make connections so that students can:

➤ link conceptual and procedural knowledge;

➤ relate various representations of concepts or procedures to one another;

➤ recognize relationships among different topics in mathematics;

➤ use mathematics in other curriculum areas;

➤ use mathematics in their daily lives.

from *Curriculum and Evaluation Standards for School Mathematics*,
National Council of Teachers of Mathematics, 1989.

APPROACHES

This standard is really two-fold: Students learn to link mathematical concepts to their everyday lives, and they learn to see how mathematical ideas are related.

Opportunities to make these connections arise throughout the school day. Looking at a map with a distance scale, for example, prior to going on a field trip to a zoo helps students figure out distances and routes. Making measurements as part of a cooking exercise connects math with preparing a meal. Studying a clock to figure out how many minutes will pass before students leave the classroom to go to the music room gives a purpose to being able to tell time. These practical applications help students see how mathematics is useful in their lives.

Students discover and can be taught that math is more than just computation and that mathematical procedures and understandings are interrelated. They soon see that multiplication is a quick way of adding and that division is related to repeated subtraction. Such understanding helps make sense of mathematics' rules and procedures and gives students a foundation on which to build a meaningful whole.

Teachers need to emphasize the importance of mathematics across the various curricular areas just as they have argued about the importance of language-arts skills in every area of the elementary curriculum. Mathematics is significant in the arts, science, and social studies. It has an equally important role in health and physical education.

Teachers and parents can help students realize these connections and cross-disciplinary applications rather than see the school day only as a collection of discrete subjects. As more elementary-school teachers work and plan in teams to teach large units of study, there is an opportunity to create this greater wholeness out of the school curriculum.

RESOURCES

These resources may help teachers and parents provide a rich mathematical environment for children. The titles under "Books" provide background reading and understanding. The books listed under "Other Resources" are primarily for student use and often contain reproducible pages. This section also lists games, manipulatives, videos, sets of materials, and computer programs. There are brief descriptions of each product. Although a supplier is listed, books may also be available directly from publishers, and books and other materials may be available from several distributors.

Although efforts were made to be thorough, this resource list is not exhaustive. There are other companies that carry many fine products. In addition, new products are constantly coming on the market, and some of the items that are included may go out of print or be discontinued in the future.

This resource list, however, provides a range of available resources for teaching mathematical connections.

Addresses of publishers and suppliers are listed in chapter 15.

Books

** Baker, Ann, and Johnny Baker. **Counting on a Small Planet: Activities for Environmental Mathematics**. Portsmouth, N.H.: Heinemann, 1991. 104p.

———. **Raps and Rhymes in Maths**. Portsmouth, N.H.: Heinemann, 1991. 90p.

Baker, Dave, Cheryl Semple, and Tony Stead. **How Big Is the Moon? Whole Maths in Action**. Portsmouth, N.H.: Heinemann, 1990. 110p.

Barry, David, adapter. **The Rajah's Rice**. New York: Scholastic, 1994. 32p.
This picture book uses an old folktale and shows the exponential factor involved in doubling grains of rice again and again.

** Burns, Marilyn, and Stephanie Sheffield. **Math and Literature**. Sausalito, Calif.: Math Solutions Publications, 1992. 80p. Grades K-3. Distributed by Cuisenaire Company of America.
This publication describes ten classroom lessons based on specific stories. It lists additional books and instructional ideas.

Burns, Marilyn, and Martha Weston. **The $1.00 Word Riddle Book**. Sausalito, Calif.: Math Solutions Publications, 1990. 48p. Distributed by Cuisenaire Company of America.

Caney, Steven. **Steven Caney's Kids' America**. New York: Workman Publishing, 1978. 416p. Grade 4 and up. Also available from Dale Seymour Publications.
This book includes stories, crafts, and recipes for individual and group activities in science, art, writing, history, and math.

Chapman, Gillian, and Pam Robson. **Maps and Mazes**. Brookfield, Conn.: Millbrook Press, 1993. 32p. Also available from Dale Seymour Publications.
Students learn map-making techniques and maze construction.

Countryman, Joan. **Writing to Learn Mathematics**. Portsmouth, N.H.: Heinemann, 1992. 101p. Grades K-12.
Samples of student writing are included.

Edwards, Deidre. **Maths in Context**. Portsmouth, N.H.: Heinemann, 1990. 148p.

Frank, Marjorie. **Math Bulletin Boards**. Nashville, Tenn.: Incentive Publications, 1986. 64p.
This publication contains 58 colorful bulletin-board ideas.

** Friedman, Aileen. **A Cloak for the Dreamer**. New York: Scholastic, 1994. Unpaged. Grades 2-4.
This picture-book story is of a tailor's sons who make cloaks using various shapes of cloth.

Gay, Sylvia, and Janet Hoelker. **Math Medley**. Nashville, Tenn.: Incentive Publications, 1992. 64p.
Hands-on activities are integrated with curricular areas.

Griffiths, Ruth, and Margaret Clyne. **Books You Can Count On: Linking Mathematics and Literature**. Portsmouth, N.H.: Heinemann, 1991. 100p.

Grossman, Virginia, and Sylvia Long. **Ten Little Rabbits**. San Francisco, Calif.: Chronicle Books, 1991. 28p. Also available from Dale Seymour Publications.
Children count from one to ten, and each number introduces a facet of Native American culture.

Hartman, Wendy. **One Sun Rises**. New York: Dutton, 1994. Unpaged.
This counting book may be used with kindergarten and first-grade students.

** = **Highly recommended.**   = **Computer resources.**   = **Videos.**

Hutchins, Pat. **The Doorbell Rang**. New York: Scholastic, 1986. 24p.
This picture book for primary grades combines reading and mathematics.

Parks, Brenda. **Something Old, Something New**. Crystal Lake, Ill.: Rigby, 1993. 95p. Grades K-3.
This book demonstrates how traditional tales can be starting points for exploring aspects of mathematics and other curriculum areas.

Rayner, Mary. **One by One, Garth Pig's Rain Song**. New York: Dutton, 1994. Unpaged.
This is a simple counting song.

Reimer, Luetta, and Wilbert Reimer. **Mathematicians Are People, Too**. Palo Alto, Calif.: Dale Seymour Publications, 1990. *Vol. 1*, 152p.; *Vol. 2*, 152p.
Stories focus on moments of discovery by great mathematicians.

Welchman-Tischler, Rosamond. **How to Use Children's Literature to Teach Mathematics**. Reston, Va.: National Council of Teachers of Mathematics, 1992. 80p. Also available from Dale Seymour Publications.
Activities promote the connection between math and children's literature.

✱✱ Whitin, David J., and Sandra Wilde. **Read Any Good Math Lately? Children's Books for Mathematical Learning K-6**. Portsmouth, N.H.: Heinemann, 1992. 206p.

Other Resources

(manipulatives, games, sets, reproducibles, videos, and computer diskettes)

Air Miles Math. Rowley, Mass.: Didax Educational Resources. Grade 3 and up.
This game uses percentages, ratios, place value, approximation, and estimation and integrates math and geography. Players travel around an illustrated game board, making purchases and collecting points.

Campaign Math. Tuscon, Ariz.: MindPlay. Computer diskette for Apple II, II Plus, IIe, IIc. Grade 3 and up. Available from NASCO.
Students playing this game learn about the election process and must use fractions, percentages, and ratios to win the election. A game booklet and teacher's guide are included.

Challenge Boxes. Palo Alto, Calif.: Dale Seymour Publications. By Catherine Valentino. 128p. Grades 4-8, gifted.
Fifty reproducible projects challenge thinking skills. Activities integrate language arts, science, social studies, math, art, and reference skills.

Consumer Math Games. Birmingham, Ala.: The Re-Print Corporation.
The following board games are available: *Bank Account*, Grades 5-12; *Budget*, Grades 4-12; *Shopping Bag*, Grades 3-8; *Primary Money Chase*, Grades K-3; *Grocery Cart*, Grades 4-9; *Department Store Math*, Grades 4-8; *Allowance*, Grades 3-8; *Purchase*, Grades 4-9; and *Fun at the Fair*, Grades 2-6.

✱✱ **CurricuLinks**. Worth, Ill.: Creative Publications. By Ann Roper, Christy Fong, and Kim Saxe. 96p. each. Grades K-6.
These books give ideas for connecting math to social studies, music, health, physical education, technology, multicultural studies, language, literature, dramatic

play, science, cooking, and art. Included are *CurricuLinks K-2, CurricuLinks 3-4,* and *CurricuLinks 5-6.* Also available as a series.

Eureka Math Components. Vernon Hills, Ill.: ETA.

This set includes storybooks available as big books and student books for Grades K-2, real-life math books for Grades 3 and 4, teacher-idea books, student activity books, and blackline masters. There is also a *Eureka Math Kit,* which includes measuring tools, classification materials, geometric models, cubes, dice, school money, and place-value manipulatives.

Grandfather Tang's Story: A Tale Told with Tangrams. New York: Crown Books for Young Readers, 1990. By Ann Tompert. Also available from Creative Publications.

This book comes with two sets of tangrams and integrates math and language arts. The watercolor illustrations are embellished with animal designs created from the tangrams.

Hands-on Math Storybooks. Blacklick, Ohio: SRA/McGraw Hill.

These storybooks help children integrate reading and mathematics through the use of stories and manipulatives. Titles include *Charlie Baker, Cookie Maker; The Emerald Forest Matching Game;* and *How Many Fish Do You See in the Sea?*

Historical Connections in Mathematics, Volume 3. Fresno, Calif.: AIMS Education Foundation. Grades 4-10.

This is the third book in a series that provides resources for linking history and mathematics. Included are biographical information, famous quotations, and anecdotes from the lives of ten mathematicians. Each chapter contains reproducible activity sheets.

Interactive Mathematics, a K-8, CD-ROM Program. Columbus, Ohio: Silver Burdett Ginn.

This program includes a *Math Processor, Animated Stories for Grades K-2, Hot Pages for Grades 3-8,* and Teacher Support Materials.

Journey to the Other Side. Worth, Ill.: Creative Publications. By Carl Sherrill.

The 240-page novel integrates math, literature, and music and appeals to students in middle grades. Comes with a teacher's guide and a 60-minute cassette tape with 16 songs that help students remember problem-solving strategies.

Learning Adventures with Sammy Spy. Torrance, Calif.: Davidson and Associates. Computer diskette for IBM compatibles. Grades 3-9. Also available from NASCO.

In following Sammy Spy's adventures, students will use knowledge of fractions, decimals, percents, sequencing, historical events, geographical locations, spelling, exchange rates, and timetables.

** **Math Excursions**. Portsmouth, N.H.: Heinemann, 1993. By Donna Burk, et al. Also available from ETA.

This series of books associates math with art, literature, science, and social studies. Each book contains five units. Available books include *Excursions K, Excursions 1,* and *Excursions 2.*

Math Theme Packs. Rowley, Mass.: Didax Educational Resources.

Each math pack includes three math games, pieces, and instructions. Pack 1 for Grades K-1 contains *Bears to the Honey, Cat and Mouse,* and *Tortoise Twelve* and deals with counting, number recognition, and addition up to 12. Pack 2 for Grades 1-2 contains *Four and Twenty Blackbirds, Journey to the Moon,* and *Tumbling Teens* and deals with grouping, addition, teens values, and the twos multiplication table. Pack 3 for Grades 1-3 contains *Paper Round, Round Up,* and *Teddy's Quilt* and reinforces thinking and strategic movements. Pack 4 for Grades 2-4 contains *Mountaineer, The Moon Game,* and *Dragon's Treasure,* which use addition, subtraction, multiplication, and division skills.

** **MEGA (Math Explorations and Group Activity) Projects**. Palo Alto, Calif.: Dale Seymour Publications. By Carole Greenes, et al.

Students work individually or in pairs from two days to two weeks to complete math projects that are connected to such other disciplines as science, art, and architecture. Includes 50 project cards for each of Grades 1-6. Includes blackline masters.

 ** **Minds on Math: A Project Approach**. Blacklick, Ohio: SRA/McGraw Hill.

Level I, Grades K-3; and *Level II,* Grades 3-4. Each level contains investigation books, lap books, activity cards, game boards, and a teacher's guide. Level II is available with *SRA's Cruncher Software* for Macintosh or IBM compatibles.

Multicultural Math Game Boards. Columbus, Ohio: Judy/Instructo.

Available separately or as *Primary Game Pack 1* and *Primary Game Pack 2,* these games are multileveled and share information about different cultures while reinforcing mathematical reasoning abilities. The front side features a game board, background information, and instructions. The reverse contains two reproducible activity sheets and notes for the teacher suggesting ways to connect the game to other curriculum areas. Games included are *Hasami Shogi, Totolospi, Yote, Shut the Box, Fox and Geese, Patol, Snakes and Ladders, Pachisi, Game of Goose,* and *Gluckshaus.* Also available in *Intermediate Game Pack 1,* which includes *Go, Kono, Tablut, Mu Torere,* and *Tric Trac;* and *Intermediate Game Pack 2,* which includes *The Royal Game of Ur, Nine Men's Morris, Senet, Alquerque,* and *Wari.*

** **Reading Books for Mathematics, Primary**. New Hyde Park, N.Y.: Learning Links. Grades K-3.

Study guide explains how to use children's literature to reinforce the mathematics curriculum. The basic set has ten titles: *Alexander Who Used to Be Rich Last Sunday; Anno's Counting Book; A Bag Full of Pups; Bunches and Bunches of Bunnies; The Doorbell Rang; How Big Is a Foot?; Rooster's Off to See the World; Thump, Thump, Rat-a-Tat-Tat; A Three Hat Day;* and *Two Ways to Count to Ten. Extra Set 1* and *Extra Set 2* are also available and each contains an additional ten titles.

Real Life Math Mysteries: A Kids' Answer to the Question, "What Will We Ever Use This For?" Pacific Grove, Calif.: Critical Thinking Press & Software. By Mary Ford Washington. 104p. Grade 3 to adult.

Scenarios are presented by a variety of working people, and math problems are drawn from their work-related experiences. Pages are reproducible.

Simulations to Stimulate Thinking. El Cajon, Calif.: Interact. Also available from Dale Seymour Publications.

This series allows students to work in groups to explore topics involving math, history, and geography. Each set contains a teacher's guide and 35 student guides. Some also contain cards and reproducible handouts. Titles include *Lost Tribe of Tocowans*, Grades 3-5; *Shopping Spree*, Grades 4-8; *Caravans*, Grades 4-8; *Gold Rush*, Grades 4-8; and *Athenian Secret*, Grades 2-5.

Stories to Solve and **More Stories to Solve**. New York: Greenwillow Books, 1985. By George Shannon. All grades. Also available from Dale Seymour Publications.

Illustrated folktales provide puzzles and mysteries to solve. Answers and notes are provided.

Teaching Primary Math with Music. Palo Alto, Calif.: Dale Seymour Publications. By Esther Mendlesohn. 96p. Grades K-3.

This book includes piano music, chords for all the songs, teaching activities, blackline masters, and an audiocassette.

** **Teaching Tessellating Art: Activities and Transparency Masters**. Palo Alto, Calif.: Dale Seymour Publications. By Jill Britton and Walter Britton. 288p.

Activities provide instruction on tessellations, making transparency masters, workshop activities, and creating tessellations with a computer.

ThemeWorks: An Integrated Curriculum for Young Children. Worth, Ill.: Creative Publications. By Joan Westley. Grades PreK-2.

Each of the books focuses on one theme and weaves together language, math, art, science, literature, music, and social studies. Titles available include *Night Time*, *Rain*, *Trees*, *Houses*, *Under the Ground*, and *At the Seashore*. The books are also available for purchase as a *Complete Program*.

Tricon Navigation: Geometry Problem Solving (and a Bit of Geography). Mount Pleasant, Mich.: Tricon Publishing, 1992. By William Swart. Grades 4-9. Also available from Dale Seymour Publications.

The kit includes navigation problems in five levels and a teacher's guide with answers and blackline masters. Students work with angles, distances and geography, and navigation problems.

Understanding Math, Integrated Language Arts: Poetry, Kit 5. Bothell, Wash.: The Wright Group, 1988. Grades K-1.

The kit includes big books, six-packs, blackline masters, and a teacher's resource book. Titles include *How Many?*; *What's the Time, Mr. Wolf?*; and *How Big Is Big?*

Understanding Math, Integrated Language Arts: Poetry, Kit 6. Bothell, Wash.: The Wright Group, 1988. Grades 1-2.

The kit includes big books, six-packs, blackline masters, and a teacher's resource book. Titles include *Soldiers* and *Ten Little Goblins*.

Understanding Math, Integrated Language Arts: Poetry, Kit 7. Bothell, Wash.: The Wright Group, 1988. Grades 2-3.

Big books, six-packs, blackline masters, and a teacher's resource book are included in this kid. Titles include *Skittles* and *Wheels*.

Windows to My World. Columbus, Ohio: Silver Burdett Ginn. Grades K-2.

This teacher resource contains a student-response book, a classroom library that consists of a collection of trade books, an audiocassette of children's songs correlated to the lessons, blackline masters, activities to link the family to the child's learning, assessment options, and a poster package. In addition to this basic set there are additional components: *Big Shared Book Package* with literature selections and activities relating to mathematics and literature; and a manipulative kit with such tools as a graphing mat, rubber stamps, pattern blocks, Cuisenaire rods, teddy bear counters, round disc counters, connections cubes, and coin sets.

Young Architects Kit. Available from Dale Seymour Publications.

Students make floor plans from acrylic templates. Kit comes with 100 assembly parts, drafting paper, and furniture tracing guides.

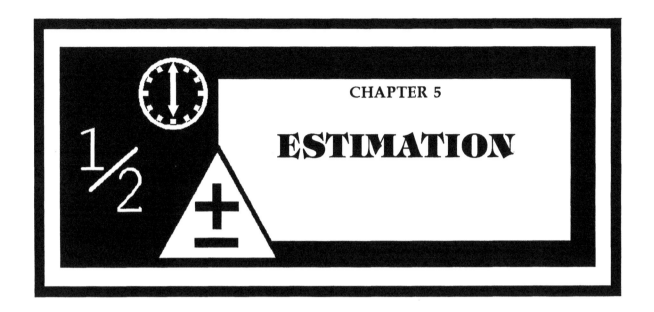

CHAPTER 5

ESTIMATION

In grades K-4, the curriculum should include estimation so students can:

➤ explore estimation strategies;

➤ recognize when an estimate is appropriate;

➤ determine the reasonableness of results;

➤ apply estimation in working with quantities, measurements, computation, and problem solving.

from *Curriculum and Evaluation Standards for School Mathematics,*
National Council of Teachers of Mathematics, 1989.

APPROACHES

Estimation is a natural part of a child's life. Students are already familiar with words such as *about, closer to,* and *nearly.* As they work with mathematics, students learn when it is appropriate to make an estimation and how close an estimate should be. They learn that they can use mathematics without always being exact.

An example a teacher might offer would be of an adult in a grocery store with only ten dollars to spend. By rounding off the price of such things as a gallon of milk, a loaf of bread, and a pound of apples, the adult estimates the price and knows whether he or she has sufficient money and roughly what the amount of change due will be. A student might be encouraged to do this and estimate the amount of change.

Such activities may add a little time to a parent's brief shopping trip. Extra time is not always available. But when it is, a child can learn and practice an important mathematical skill in a natural setting with a minimum of fuss and bother.

It is important that students see that estimation plays a legitimate part in mathematics. Students might pace off the length and width of a room and, by measuring their stride, come up with an estimate of the number of square feet of carpet.

Another student, who has divided 100 by 13 and is not sure if her or his answer is correct might consider that 100 divided by ten is ten, so 100 divided by 13 must be a number smaller than ten.

These rough guesses, or estimates, can help students detect a serious error made in a calculation and can help them determine when an answer for a problem seems reasonable. A variety of estimating skills can be taught, and there will be numerous opportunities to show that estimation plays a valuable part in everyday school situations.

RESOURCES

These resources may help teachers and parents provide a rich mathematical environment for children. The titles under "Books" provide background reading and understanding. The books listed under "Other Resources" are primarily for student use and often contain reproducible pages. The section also lists games, manipulatives, videos, sets of materials, and computer programs. There are brief descriptions of each product. Although a supplier is listed, books may also be available directly from publishers, and books and other materials may be available from several distributors.

Although efforts were made to be thorough, this resource list is not exhaustive. There are other companies that carry many fine products. In addition, new products are constantly coming on the market, and some of the items that are included may go out of print or be discontinued in the future.

This resource list, however, provides a range of available resources for teaching estimation.

Addresses of publishers and suppliers are listed in chapter 15.

Books

Fair, Jan, and Mary Melvin. **Kids Are Consumers Too! Real-World Mathematics for Today's Classroom**. Reading, Mass.: Addison Wesley Longman, 1986. 304p. Grades 3-8. Also available from Dale Seymour Publications.

This book contains more than 100 activities, including many that involve estimation.

** Lee, Marty, and Marcia Miller. **Estimation Investigations: More Than 65 Activities That Build Mathematical Reasoning and Number Sense**. New York: Scholastic Professional Books, 1995. 80p. Grades 4-6. Also available from Institute for Math Mania.

This book is filled with investigations that challenge students to develop their estimation skills.

** Shoen, Harold L., ed. **Estimation and Mental Computation**. Reston, Va.: National Council of Teachers of Mathematics, 1986. 248p.

Stenmark, J., V. Thompson, and R. Cossey. **Family Math**. Berkeley, Calif.: University of California, Lawrence Hall of Science, 1986. 319p. Grades K-8. Also available from Dale Seymour Publications.

Available in Spanish and English versions, this book contains 100 hands-on activities involving estimation and using calculators, computers, logical thinking, geometry, statistics, and measurement.

Van de Walle, John A. **Elementary School Mathematics: Teaching Developmentally**. 2d ed. White Plains, N.Y.: Longman, 1994. 544p.
Chapter 11 discusses estimation.

** Welchman-Tischler, Rosamond. **The Mathematical Toolbox**. White Plains, N.Y.: Cuisenaire Company of America, 1992. 90p.

This book contains more than 200 math challenges that integrate a variety of manipulatives. Students use Cuisenaire rods, cubes, and other manipulatives for estimation as well as for counting, working with fractions, and determining probability.

Williams, David E. **Creative Mathematics Teaching with Calculators**. Sunnyvale, Calif.: Stokes Publishing, 1992. 112p. All grades. Also available from Dale Seymour Publications.

This book's investigations use calculators to develop skill in estimation, mental math, problem solving, and number sense.

Other Resources

(manipulatives, games, sets, reproducibles, videos, and computer diskettes)

Ballpark Figures. Birmingham, Ala.: The Re-Print Corporation.

This game reinforces estimating skills. On the reverse of the game board are *Prehistoric Times* and *Dinosaur Division*, which build multiplication and division skills.

Challenge: A Program for the Mathematically Talented. Palo Alto, Calif.: Dale Seymour Publications. By V. Haag, B. Kaufman, E. Martin, and G. Rising. Grades 3-6.

This four-volume series for advanced learners includes exercises in estimation, logical thinking, strategic reasoning, and problem solving. For each volume there is a teacher's edition and a student workbook. Also available is a manipulative kit which includes minicomputer boards, magnetic checkers, and string games for all levels.

** **A Collection of Math Lessons from Grades 3 Through 6**. Sausalito, Calif.: Math Solutions Publications, 1987. By Marilyn Burns. 174p. Distributed by Cuisenaire Company of America.

This collection contains lessons on estimation, statistics, spatial relationships, and operations.

Constructing Ideas About Large Numbers. Worth, Ill.: Creative Publications. By Julie Pier Brodie. 112p. Grades 3-6.

This book contains reproducibles. The investigations require the use of manipulatives to explore estimation, place value, and problem solving with large

---

** = **Highly recommended.**   = **Computer resources.**   = **Videos.**

numbers. Also available are a *Starter Set*, which includes enough materials for eight students working in pairs, and a *Classroom Kit*, with materials for 32 students working in pairs.

Estimate! Calculate! Evaluate! White Plains, N.Y.: Cuisenaire Company of America, 1990. By Marjorie W. Bloom and Grace K. Galton. 88p. Grades 5-8.
This set contains 37 reproducible math work sheets and activities.

Estimation: Quick Solve I. Minneapolis, Minn.: MECC/Softkey International. Computer diskette for Apple II series. Grades 5-8. Also available from NASCO.
Students practice visual and computational estimation skills.

Estimation Exploration. Hayward, Calif.: Activity Resources Company, 1994. By Tom Murray. 64p. Grades 3-8. Also available from ETA.
Hands-on activities for thinking, writing, and talking about estimation are included. Contains teaching suggestions and extension ideas.

Estimeasure: Estimation and Measurement Activities. Palo Alto, Calif.: Dale Seymour Publications. 144p. Grades 3-8.
This material provides hands-on experience in linear and area measurement and estimation. Includes blackline masters. Titles available are *Estimeasure Book*, *Right-Angle Polygons*, *Triangles/Other Polygons*, *Circles/Parts of Circles*, and *Irregular Shapes*.

Exploring with Color Tiles. White Plains, N.Y.: Cuisenaire Company of America, 1990. By Sandra Mogensen and Judi Magarian-Gold. 96p. Grades PreK-6.
This book and its overhead-projector activities help students explore estimation as well as patterns, counting, place value, number facts, probability, and measurement. Available separately are *Color Tiles*, which come in sets of 400 tiles in four colors, and *Color Squares for the Overhead Projector*, a 50-piece set of transparent squares in ten colors.

Guess. Palo Alto, Calif.: Dale Seymour Publications. By Robert Reys and Barbara Reys. Grades 4-12.
Each Guess box contains 105 cards for teaching estimation strategies. Available in two different boxes or as a set.

Making Numbers Make Sense. Reading, Mass.: Addison Wesley Longman, 1993. By Ronald Ritchart. 144p. Grades K-8.
This resource book suggests projects and evaluation ideas and includes blackline masters. The lessons cover many areas, including estimation, measurement, place value, and calculators.

Math Blaster: In Search of Spot. Torrance, Calif.: Davidson and Associates. Grades 1-6. Also available from Egghead Software.
This computer game gives students practice in estimation, fractions, decimals, percents, and in using addition, subtraction, multiplication, and division.

Measure Works. Minneapolis, Minn.: MECC/Softkey International. Computer diskette for Apple II, II Plus, IIe, IIc, IIgs. Grades 1-4. Also available from NASCO.
Students learn to compare sizes and heights and to measure with whole units. They also gain comfort in making estimations before making exact calculations. Comes with a teacher's guide.

** **Mental Math and Estimation**. White Plains, N.Y.: Cuisenaire Company of America, 1992. By Don Miller. 80p. Grades 3-8.

Activities improve mental math and estimation skills and can be produced on overhead transparency or as student copies. A calculator (not included) is integral to the lessons.

Mental Math and Estimation. Blacklick, Ohio: SRA/McGraw Hill. Grades 3-9.

This ten-lesson program provides instruction and practice in mental computation with multiples of ten, 100, and 1,000.

** **Number Sense, Numeration and Estimation Kit**. Vernon Hills: Ill.: ETA. Grades K-4.

This kit contains materials for a class of 20 to 30 students. The activities help develop basic number concepts by using a variety of mathematical models. Contains such manipulatives as number lines, number cubes, counters, Peg-Boards, sorting trays, links, Versa-Tiles, and resource books.

 See You Later Estimator Video I. Watertown, Mass.: Tom Snyder Productions. Grades K-2. Also available from Creative Publications.

This video contains four games in which students estimate and share guesses. Also available is *See You Later Estimator Video II*, Grades 3-4, which contains four games to encourage verbal sharing of the strategies used to estimate numbers.

Think About It! Primary Math Problems of the Day. Worth, Ill.: Creative Publications. By Marcy Cook. 96p. Grades 1-3.

This book contains 360 math puzzles involving such skills as estimation, arithmetic, and choosing the correct operation. *Think About It! Mathematics Activities of the Day*, Grades 4-8, contains a variety of math challenges.

Tic-Tac-Toe Math. Palo Alto, Calif.: Dale Seymour Publications. By Dave Clark. 112p. Grades 5-9.

Reproducible problems in a tic-tac-toe-game format explore such concepts as time, money, fractions, estimation, decimals, geometry, and statistics.

Two-Color Counters. Palo Alto, Calif.: Dale Seymour Publications.

A set of 200 counters that are red on one side and yellow on the other can be used for estimation, matching, probability, and so on. Comes with an activity booklet. Also available are *Overhead Counters*.

CHAPTER 6

NUMBER SENSE AND NUMERATION

In grades K-4, the curriculum should include whole number concepts and skills so that students can:

➤ construct number meanings through real-world experiences and the use of physical materials;

➤ understand our numeration system by relating counting, grouping, and place-value concepts;

➤ develop number sense;

➤ interpret the multiple uses of numbers encountered in the real world.

from *Curriculum and Evaluation Standards for School Mathematics,*
National Council of Teachers of Mathematics, 1989.

APPROACHES

Young children need many opportunities to develop their understanding of numbers. They will find reasons to count and to represent numbers using a variety of manipulatives. They also must come to understand place value so that they can work comfortably with single-digit and multidigit number ideas.

It takes time to develop good number concepts. This valuable foundation is best prepared in the early years of schooling and with numbers that have meaning for students. Students may have the task of keeping track of the number of school days and holding a special 100 day to celebrate that landmark. Students may also be asked to bring in 100 of some thing, such as 100 grains of rice, 100 dried peas, or a sheet of wrapping paper decorated with 100 polka dots. As students share and discuss these items, they become familiar with the concept of 100.

Gradually they come to understand larger numbers; the meaning of ordinal and cardinal numbers; the relationships among numbers, such as 60 being six tens or eight being one more than seven; the relative magnitude of numbers; and the effects of performing such operations on numbers as addition and division. They also develop referents for measurements used in everyday situations and come to understand, for example, that ground meat would not be $298 a pound.

Place value is critical, and it takes time for students to develop their understandings. They need many experiences in comparing, ordering, rounding, and operating with larger numbers. They may count sticks or buttons or other objects by ones and then group them into piles of tens and still have some left over. Various manipulatives are particularly helpful in exploring number relationships.

RESOURCES

These resources may help teachers and parents provide a rich mathematical environment for children. The titles under "Books" provide background reading and understanding. The books listed under "Other Resources" are primarily for student use and often contain reproducible pages. This section also lists games, manipulatives, videos, sets of materials, and computer programs. There are brief descriptions of each product. Although a supplier is listed, books may also be available directly from publishers, and books and other materials may be available from several distributors.

Although efforts were made to be thorough, this resource list is not exhaustive. There are other companies that carry many fine products. In addition, new products are constantly coming on the market, and some of the items that are included may go out of print or be discontinued in the future.

This resource list, however, provides a range of available resources for teaching number sense and numeration.

Addresses of publishers and suppliers are listed in chapter 15.

Books

Burk, Donna, Allyn Snider, and Paula Symonds. **Math Excursions Series, K, 1, 2**. Portsmouth, N.H.: Heinemann, 1992. *K*, 266p.; *1*, 259p.; and *2*, 218p.

** Burns, Marilyn. "The Shapes of Math." Part 2 of **Math for Smarty Pants**. Boston: Little, Brown, 1982. 128p.

Chwast, Seymour. **The 12 Circus Rings**. San Diego, Calif.: Harcourt Brace Jovanovich, 1993. Unpaged.

Kaye, Peggy. **Games for Math**. New York: Pantheon Books, 1987. 236p.
This book includes a section on counting and the number system.

Kelleher, Heather J. **Mathworks Book B**. Boston: Houghton Mifflin, 1992. 400p.
This book contains a useful section for primary grades on place value.

** Lee, Marty, and Marcia Miller. **Estimation Investigations: More Than 65 Activities That Build Mathematical Reasoning and Number Sense**. New York: Scholastic Professional Books, 1995. 80p. Grades 4-6. Also available from Institute for Math Mania.

Spann, Mary Beth. **Exploring the Numbers One to One Hundred: Activities, Learning Center Ideas and Celebrations, Grades PreK-2**. Jefferson City, Mo.: Scholastic Professional Books, 1995. 48p.

** Van de Walle, John A. **Elementary School Mathematics: Teaching Developmentally**. 2d ed. White Plains, N.Y.: Longman, 1994. 544p.
Chapter 6 is especially useful to the topic of numeration.

Other Resources
(manipulatives, games, sets, reproducibles, videos, and computer diskettes)

Attribute Beads. Birmingham, Ala.: The Re-Print Corporation.
A set includes 144 beads in four shapes, three sizes, and six colors. Also available are sets of *Circular Sorting Trays* and *Attribute Bead Activity Cards*, which come with teacher's notes for 64 activities of varying complexity.

Attribute Buttons. Boulder, Colo.: PlayFair Toys. Grades PreK-1.
This set of 50 jumbo buttons in different sizes, thicknesses, textures, and colors comes with a storage tub. The buttons have between one and ten holes.

Base Ten Blocks. Columbus, Ohio: Judy/Instructo.
Plastic base ten blocks are available separately or in sets of four.

** **Base Ten Blocks**. Worth, Ill.: Creative Publications. Grades K-8.
Base ten blocks are available in hardwood or in yellow plastic. They can be purchased by units, tens, hundreds, and thousands and in sets such as *Bucket of Base Ten Blocks, Introductory Set of Base Ten Blocks, Base Ten Blocks Primary Classroom Set, Base Ten Blocks Intermediate Classroom Set, Base Ten Blocks for the Overhead, Base Ten Blocks Sampler,* and *Base Ten Rubber Stamps*. Kathryn Walker and Kelly Steward's *20 Thinking Questions for Base Ten Blocks* contains 20 activities with base ten blocks and may be used by students working with partners. One book is available for Grades 2-3; another for Grades 3-6. Each contains 112 pages. These books can also be purchased as kits with manipulatives and contain enough materials for a class of 32 students working in pairs.

** **Base Ten Blocks**. Buffalo, N.Y.: SI Manufacturing Limited.
Base ten blocks provide concrete models to give meaning to place value, operations of whole numbers, and decimals. Available in various units with cubes, rods, flats, mats, and a teacher's guide.

Base Ten Cubes. Richardson, Tex.: Kaidy Educational Resources.
These cubes can be used to help students explore the relationship of numbers in the base ten system. Available are packages of cubes and rods of plastic, plain paper cubes, and a book, *Base Ten Mathematics*, by Mary Laycock, Grades K-8, 64p., which provides sample problems.

Base 10 Dominoes Set. Columbus, Ohio: Judy/Instructo.

Using 64 dominoes and matching number symbols, words, and models, students grasp the basics of place value from one to 500.

Base 10 Group Set. Columbus, Ohio: Judy/Instructo.

In sufficient quantities for ten to 15 children, the set includes 300 plastic units, 100 rods, and 25 flats. Individual pieces are also available separately.

Base Ten Resource Materials Set. Rowley, Mass.: Didax Educational Resources.

The complete set contains 200 one-centimeter cubes, 100 ten-centimeter rods, 30 ten-centimeter flats, and four ten-centimeter blocks. Additional packages of blocks, flats, rods, and cubes are available.

** **Base 10 Set**. Columbus, Ohio: Judy/Instructo. Grades 1-4.

The set includes 30 activities, 45 activity cards, 300 units, 100 rods, and 25 flats with two levels of problem-solving activities. *Activity cards* are available separately.

Beginning Base 10 Flannelboard Set. Columbus, Ohio: Judy/Instructo.

The set includes 45 units, ten rods, one flat, and place-value cards.

Beginning Base Ten Set. Birmingham, Ala.: The Re-Print Corporation.

With enough materials for 15 students, the set includes cubes, rods, and flats. Also available are *Base Ten Number Concept Set, Base Ten Place Value Paper, Base Ten Small Group Numeration Kit, Base Ten Large Group Numeration Kit,* and *Base Ten Block for the Overhead Projector.*

Clear View Base Ten Block Starter Set. Birmingham, Ala.: The Re-Print Corporation. Grade K and up.

These can be bought as a set or as separate components. They are transparent, interlocking blocks that allow students to look through number values while building rods out of cubes and so on. Also available are *Clear View Base Ten Activity Cards* for counting and showing numbers.

Constructing Ideas About Counting: Grades 1-3. Worth, Ill.: Creative Publications. By Sandra Ward. 112p.

This book contains activities involving manipulatives and includes reproducible pages.

Counting Frames. Birmingham, Ala.: The Re-Print Corporation.

A variety of frames are available in plastic and wood. They range from five rods of ten beads each to ten rods of ten beads each with ½-inch to one-inch beads.

Counting People. Palo Alto, Calif.: Dale Seymour Publications.

These freestanding male and female plastic figures in red, blue, green, and yellow come in sets of 96 figures and in three sizes. They can be used in a variety of sorting possibilities. Also available are *Overhead People.*

** **Cubes**. Worth, Ill.: Creative Publications. Grade K and up.

A variety of cubes are available, including *Unifix Cubes, Linker Cubes, Centimeter Connecting Cubes, Rainbow Centimeter Cubes,* and large *Wooden Cubes.* Also available are *Unifix Cubes for the Overhead Projector; Primary Jobcards: Patterns with Unifix Cubes,* a set of 21 task cards; *Hands-on Unifix Cubes;* and a 144-page book of reproducible lessons.

Dinosaur and Frog Counters. Worth, Ill.: Creative Publications. Grades PreK-3.

These plastic counters are one inch tall and come in four colors. They are available in sets of 100 and buckets of 300.

Discovery Kits, Sorting & Counting. Buffalo, N.Y.: SI Manufacturing Limited.

A student set consists of a teacher's guide and 40 plastic animals, fruits, vegetables, and vehicles for sorting and counting. Also available are *Hex-a-link Cubes* in ten colors.

Hands-on Base Ten Blocks. Worth, Ill.: Creative Publications. 144p. Grades K-3.

This activity book includes reproducible lessons and puzzles. It can be purchased as a *Starter Set* with 100 cubes, 50 rods, 25 flats, and one block or as a *Hands-on Base Ten Blocks Class Set* with enough materials for 20 to 30 students working in pairs.

Hundreds Boards. Buffalo, N.Y.: SI Manufacturing Limited.

These two-sided hundreds boards measure 30 centimeters by 28 centimeters and are made of plastic-coated cardboard with tiles. A teacher's guide is included.

Kindergarten Jobcards: Count & Color with Learning Links. Worth, Ill.: Creative Publications. By Ann Roper. Grades PreK-K.

This set of 22 cards helps young children practice color recognition, matching, and counting skills. Sold separately are *Learning Links*, which are brightly colored plastic links that join and separate easily. Links are 1⅝-inch-by-¾-inch and are sold in sets of various quantities.

Luxboards. Buffalo, N.Y.: SI Manufacturing Limited. Developed at Lakehead University by Gerry Vervoort.

These concrete models of numbers emphasize the base ten system and are available with workbooks and teacher's notes.

Making Numbers Make Sense. Reading, Mass.: Addison Wesley Longman, 1993. By Ron Ritchart. 144p. Grades K-8. Also available from Dale Seymour Publications.

The lessons help students develop number sense. Blackline masters are included with the materials.

Math Balance. Rowley, Mass.: Didax Educational Resources.

The set includes a plastic balance and 20 ten-gram weights, self-adhesive labels, and an instruction booklet. Students experience the meaning of number values by placing weights on the balance. A teacher's guide is available.

Math Big Box. Blacklick, Ohio: SRA/McGraw Hill. Grades K-1.

This ready-to-use math-interest center includes place-value stamps, shape templates, games, cubes, tangram and puzzle cards, pegs, and peg board. These hands-on activities teach fundamental processes such as numeration, computation, geometry, and measurement readiness.

Math by All Means. Place Value: Grades 1-2. Sausalito, Calif.: Math Solutions Publications, 1994. By Marilyn Burns. Distributed by Cuisenaire Company of America.

Students explore the number system. There are suggestions for individual and small-group activities. Blackline masters are included.

** Math Discoveries with Base 10. Montpelier, Vt.: Institute for Math Mania. 64p.
This book of reproducibles helps students develop an understanding of place value.

Number Bingo and **Number Lotto**. Columbus, Ohio: Judy/Instructo.
In the bingo game students match sets of objects with the numbers one through 20. Includes eight bingo cards as well as calling cards, markers, and a teacher's guide. In the lotto game, which includes boards, picture cards, and a teacher's guide, students match numbers one through 20.

Number Inlays Puzzle. Columbus, Ohio: Judy/Instructo.
The 9-inch-by-12-inch wooden puzzle includes numbers zero through nine.

Number Plaques. Birmingham, Ala.: The Re-Print Corporation. Grades PreK-1.
Ten fit-in-number plaques teach recognition and counting. Made of thick crepe foam rubber, the plaques are 3½ inches by eight inches by 3⁄16-inch thick.

Number Worm Puzzle. Columbus, Ohio: Judy/Instructo.
This all-wooden worm puzzle shows numbers one through 12 as a sequencing aid.

Numberite, 1-10 and **1-20**. Columbus, Ohio: Judy/Instructo.
Wooden panels fit together in numerical order with insert wooden pegs to show corresponding number values. Includes a teacher's guide.

Numbers 1-20 Puzzle. Columbus, Ohio: Judy/Instructo.
The colorful 12-inch-by-19-inch puzzle reinforces counting skills.

Objects for Sorting and Counting. Omaha, Nebr.: Oriental Trading Company.
This company supplies large-quantity amounts of inexpensive, small plastic animals, chenille stems, stickers, and so on. All may be used for a variety of activities in counting and sorting.

Objects for Sorting and Counting. Grandview, Mo.: U.S. Toy Company.
This company supplies in packages of a dozen or more many small, inexpensive items such as dogs and dinosaurs that may be used for various activities in grouping and sorting.

100 Bears Floor Puzzle. Columbus, Ohio: Judy/Instructo. Grades PreK-3.
This two-foot-by-three-foot puzzle of 50 pieces has more than 800 things to count. A teacher's guide is included.

100 Number Board. Rowley, Mass.: Didax Educational Resources.
The set includes a sturdy 11½-inch square plastic board with 100 recessed and numbered squares, 200 number tiles, and an instructional booklet.

1-10 Basic Rods and Counters. Rowley, Mass.: Didax Educational Resources.
The set includes ten numbered platforms with ten rods that will hold the correct number of beads for that platform. The platforms can be used separately or locked together to form a continuous strip. There are 55 beads in ten colors.

Place Value Board. Birmingham, Ala.: The Re-Print Corporation. Grade 1 and up.
The kit helps students learn to read and write numbers in billions. Included are comma and decimal-point inserts and a detailed instruction book.

Place Value Group Set. Rowley, Mass.: Didax Educational Resources.

The set contains 100 yellow cubes, 50 green rods, 30 blue flats, and four red blocks. It is also available in a smaller version, *Place Value Number Structure Set*.

Puzzle, Wooden 1-2-3. Boulder, Colo.: PlayFair Toys.

This 16-inch-by-12-inch puzzle has a corresponding number of dots under each of the number pieces and is used to help young children learn to count.

Radial Sorting Tray. Rowley, Mass.: Didax Educational Resources.

The tray is 12 inches in diameter with a center well and 12 surrounding compartments. Trays come singly or in packages of five and are available in blue or white. Bags of 80 *Plastic Shapes* are also available for sorting and classifying and include two each of the four colors for the ten objects.

Rainbow Bear Counters. Columbus, Ohio: Judy/Instructo.

The set includes 300 one-inch plastic bears for grouping, sorting, and counting activities. There are 50 bears in each of the following colors: red, yellow, blue, green, orange, and purple.

Sorting and Counting Kits and Guides. Buffalo, N.Y.: SI Manufacturing Limited.

These kits include trays, replicas of common objects, and a teacher's guide. Objects for sorting include fruits, vegetables, animals, and vehicles.

Sorting and Order Kit. Rowley, Mass.: Didax Educational Resources.

This kit contains two sorting trays with eight compartments and hundreds of colorful pieces of sorting materials. Sorting trays are also available separately.

Sorting Materials. Worth, Ill.: Creative Publications. Grades K-6.

Available for sorting are the following collections: *Shells*, *Buttons*, *Creepy Crawlers*, *Tiles*, *Beads*, *Nuts & Washers*, *Screw & Bolts*, and *Rocks & Pebbles*. They are also available as a *Deluxe Set*. Kathryn Walker and Kelly Stewart's *20 Thinking Questions for Sorting Treasures: Grades 1-3* is a 112-page book of investigations. It's available with manipulatives for 32 students in a *Classroom Kit* or for eight students in a *Starter Set*.

** **Teddy Bear Counters**. Worth, Ill.: Creative Publications.

The Teddy Bear Counters are one inch tall and come in four colors in sets of 100 and 300. Also available are *Teddy Bear Counters for the Overhead Projector* and individual sets of *Teddy Bear Jobcards for Counting, Adding, Subtracting*, and as a complete *Series*. These Jobcards for Grades K-1, by Micaelia Randolph Brummett and Linda Charles, help students learn simple math concepts. *The Teddy Bear Primary Classroom Kit* contains counters, counters for the overhead, Jobcards, and three books: *Story Problems with Teddy Bear Counters, Reasoning with Teddy Bear Counters,* and *Story Writing with Teddy Bear Counters*.

** **Understanding Place Value**. Worth, Ill.: Creative Publications. By Micaelia Randolph Brummett and Linda Holden Charles.

Understanding Place Value: Addition & Subtraction, Grades 2-4, and *Understanding Place Value: Multiplication & Division*, Grades 3-6, demonstrate teaching place-value skills using base ten blocks. The 128-page books can also be purchased as a set, and the following support materials are available: *Understanding Place Value Box*, with materials for two to four students; *Addition and Subtraction Small*

Group Set; Multiplication and Division Small Group Set; Understanding Place Value Complete Classroom Kit; Cooperative Problem Solving with Base Ten Blocks; and *Cooperative Problem Solving with Base Ten Blocks Class Set.*

Used Numbers Units. Counting: Ourselves and Our Family. Palo Alto, Calif.: Dale Seymour Publications. By Antonia Stone and Susan Jo Russell. Grades K-1.

Students discuss, sort, group, and display collected data. Also available is *Sorting: Groups and Graphs,* by Susan Jo Russell and Rebecca B. Corwin. Students collect, sort, and classify materials, and then construct graphs to display the results.

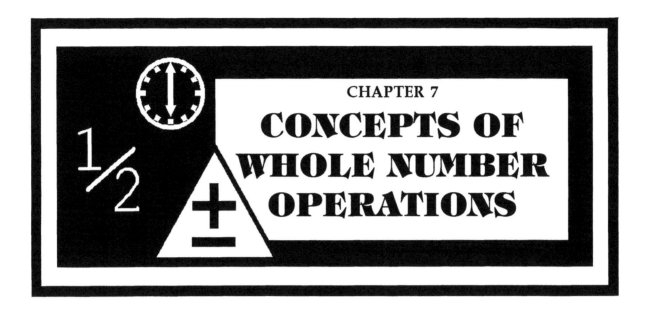

CHAPTER 7

CONCEPTS OF WHOLE NUMBER OPERATIONS

In grades K-4, the mathematics curriculum should include concepts of addition, subtraction, multiplication, and division of whole numbers so that students can:

➤ develop meaning for the operations by modeling and discussing a rich variety of problem situations;

➤ relate the mathematical language and symbolism of operations to problem situations and informal language;

➤ recognize that a wide variety of problem structures can be represented by a single operation;

➤ develop operation sense.

from *Curriculum and Evaluation Standards for School Mathematics*,
National Council of Teachers of Mathematics, 1989.

APPROACHES

Standard 7 and Standard 8, cited at the opening of chapter 8, are probably the standards most familiar to teachers, parents, and many students. Our school mathematics curriculum has always emphasized adding, subtracting, multiplying, and dividing. These are fundamental operations. Although computation is emphasized in Standard 8, Standard 7 emphasizes the development of an operation sense by focusing on concepts and relationships. Such understanding helps students know which operation to apply in any given situation.

Understanding operations includes recognizing situations when an operation would be useful, building an awareness of models of an operation, seeing relationships among operations, and having insight as to the effect of an operation on a pair of numbers.

Students need to become familiar with such mathematical terms as *addend, sum, difference, factor, multiple, product,* and *quotient.* Understanding the language of mathematics is the natural result of exploring and investigating with numbers.

Students should be asked to solve word problems and create problems for others to solve. These tasks help them understand the properties of an operation and learn, for example, that three plus nine equals 12 just as nine plus three equals 12, noting that reversing the order of two addends does not change the sum. They also gain insights on the effects of two different operations, such as the difference between adding ten to a number and multiplying a number by ten.

RESOURCES

These resources may help teachers and parents provide a rich mathematical environment for children. The titles under "Books" provide background reading and understanding. The books listed under "Other Resources" are primarily for student use and often contain reproducible pages. This section also lists games, manipulatives, videos, sets of materials, and computer programs. There are brief descriptions of each product. Although a supplier is listed, books may also be available directly from publishers, and books and other materials may be available from several distributors.

Although efforts were made to be thorough, this resource list is not exhaustive. There are other companies that carry many fine products. In addition, new products are constantly coming on the market, and some of the items that are included may go out of print or be discontinued in the future.

This resource list, however, provides a range of available resources for teaching the concepts of whole number operations.

Addresses of publishers and suppliers are listed in chapter 15.

Books

Dutton, Wilbur H. **Mathematics Children Use and Understand: Preschool Through Third Grade**. Mountain View, Calif.: Mayfield Publishing, 1991. 330p.

✱✱ Frank, Marjorie. **The Kids' Stuff Book of Math for the Primary Grades**. Nashville, Tenn.: Incentive Publications, 1988. 240p. Grades 1-3.
This book is filled with high-interest activities.

Kaye, Peggy. **Games for Math**. New York: Pantheon Books, 1987. 236p.
Games involving addition, subtraction, multiplication, and division are included.

Kelleher, Heather J. **Mathworks Book B**. Boston: Houghton Mifflin, 1992. 400p.
This book includes activities on operations, place values, and working with two-digit problems.

Schwartz, David M., and Steven Kellogg. **How Much Is a Million? Big Book Edition**. New York: William Morrow, 1994. 44p. Grades 1-4. Also available from Dale Seymour Publications.

A magician uses simple terms to introduce concepts of million, billion, and trillion.

———— . **If You Made a Million**. New York: Lothrop, Lee & Shepard, 1989. 40p. Grades 1-5. Also available from Dale Seymour Publications.
This book introduces jobs in which people earn from one penny to one million dollars.

** Van de Walle, John A. **Elementary School Mathematics: Teaching Developmentally**. 2d ed. White Plains, N.Y.: Longman, 1994. 544p.
Chapter 9 is of particular interest.

Other Resources

(manipulatives, games, sets, reproducibles, videos, and computer diskettes)

Clear View Small Group Addition/Subtraction Kit. Birmingham, Ala.: The Re-Print Corporation.
This kit includes cards, cubes, rods, and flats in sufficient quantity for two to four students to use. Also available are *Clear View Small Group Multiplication/Division Kit*, with materials for two to four students; and *Clear View Large Group Operations Kit*, which has materials for ten to 15 students. *Clear View Base Ten Activity Cards* for addition, subtraction, multiplication, and division are also available with blackline masters.

** **Constructing Ideas About Multiplication and Division: Grades 3-6**. Worth, Ill.: Creative Publications. By Julie Pier Brodie. 112p.
These investigations allow students to use manipulatives to understand multiplication and division. It's also available as a *Classroom Kit* with enough materials for 32 students to work together in pairs and as a *Starter Set* with enough materials for eight students to work in pairs.

** **Constructing Ideas About Number Combinations: Grades 1-3**. Worth, Ill.: Creative Publications. By Sandra Ward. 112p.
Activities require students to use manipulatives to explore numbers. Reproducibles are included. Also available as a *Classroom Kit* with enough materials for 32 students working in pairs or as a *Starter Set* with enough materials for eight students working in pairs.

** **Developing Number Concepts Using Unifix Cubes**. Reading, Mass.: Addison Wesley Longman, 1984. By Kathy Richardson. Also available from Dale Seymour Publications.
This book helps teachers develop number concepts by using unifix cubes. More than 75 blackline masters are included.

Experiences in Math for Young Children. Albany, N.Y.: Delmar Publishers, 1978. By R. Charlesworth and D. Radeloff. 450p. Grades K-3.
The book's sequenced activities support the construction of essential math concepts and skills. Involves concrete materials and explorations.

** = Highly recommended.   = **Computer resources.**   = **Videos.**

Floor Numbers. Rowley, Mass.: Didax Educational Resources.

The nine-centimeter cutout floor tiles are felt covered with a nonslip rubber backing. More than 70 numbers and arithmetic signs are included in the set.

 In Search of the Missing Numbers for Addition and Subtraction. Vernon Hills, Ill.: ETA. Grades K-3.

This 60-minute video builds and reinforces addition and subtraction skills as used in everyday situations.

Junior Arithmetic Squares. Rowley, Mass.: Didax Educational Resources.

This set contains 54 brightly colored squares that are printed with numbers zero through nine and operational signs. Each carpet-faced, rubber-backed square measures 6½ inches by 6½ inches.

 Math Rabbit. Fremont, Calif.: The Learning Company. Computer diskettes for Apple II, II Plus, IIe, IIc, IIgs. Grades K-2. Available from NASCO.

This computer program builds early math skills and increases students' understanding of numbers. At the most advanced level, students add and subtract two-digit numbers.

Mathematics Games for Fun and Practice. Reading, Mass.: Addison-Wesley. By Alan Barson. 88p. Grades 4-8.

Thirty-eight games reinforce understanding of basic computations, fractions, decimals, and more. Games are designed for two players.

Mathematics in Process. Portsmouth, N.H.: Heinemann, 1990. By Ann Baker and Johnny Baker. 170p. Grades K-3.

This book uses language-arts principles such as brainstorming in preparation for actual problem solving.

Multilink Beginning Math Concepts Kit. Boulder, Colo.: PlayFair Toys. Grades 1-4.

The kit contains more than 100 suggested activities for early math skills. It contains 100 cubes, ten prisms, activity cards, and a teacher's guide. Games, puzzles, and mind teasers are included.

 ** **Number Munchers**. Minneapolis, Minn.: MECC/Softkey International. Two computer diskettes for Apple II, II Plus, IIe, IIc, IIgs. Grade 3 and up. Also available from NASCO.

Students using this computer game help the Munchers hunt for numbers or numerical expressions while watching out for the Troggles. Teacher options provide a high degree of instructional control.

1-100 Activity Book. Vernon Hills, Ill.: ETA. By D. Bacarella. 80p. Grades 1-4.

This activity book contains 80 pages of reproducibles to help students enhance number concepts. Also available as an *Activity Kit* with opaque and transparent counters and a demonstration board.

Operation Magic Tricks. Pacific Grove, Calif.: Critical Thinking Press & Software. By Ronald Edwards. Grades 2-7.

These mathematical tricks lead students through a variety of computations and mathematical discoveries. Teacher instructions are included, and blackline masters are provided.

Primary Math Video. Vernon Hills, Ill.: ETA. Grades PreK-5.

This 58-minute video demonstrates the basics of primary addition, subtraction, multiplication, and division.

The Random House Audio Mathematics Program. Blacklick, Ohio: SRA/McGraw Hill. Grades 3-6.

This program provides audiocassettes and reproducible work sheets on math concepts, computation, geometry, and measurement at each grade level.

Readiness. Birmingham, Ala.: The Re-Print Corporation. Grades PreK-K.

The two-sided game board uses koala bears and parrots to aid in practicing number recognition, counting, and simple addition skills.

 Story of Numbers and What They Mean. Vernon Hills, Ill.: ETA. Grades K-1.

This 30-minute video introduces young students to numbers.

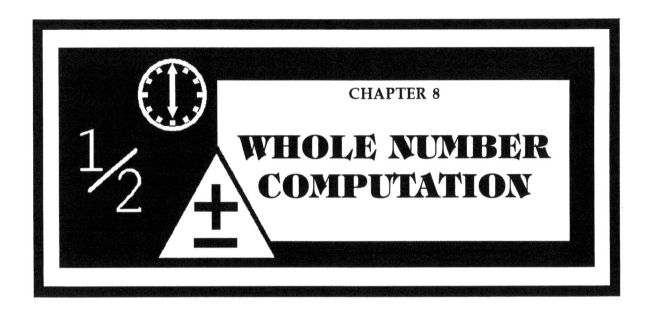

CHAPTER 8

WHOLE NUMBER COMPUTATION

In grades K-4, the mathematics curriculum should develop whole number computation so that students can:

➤ model, explain, and develop reasonable proficiency with basic facts and algorithms;

➤ use a variety of mental computation and estimation techniques;

➤ use calculators in appropriate computational situations;

➤ select and use computation techniques appropriate to specific problems and determine whether the results are reasonable.

from *Curriculum and Evaluation Standards for School Mathematics*,
National Council of Teachers of Mathematics, 1989.

APPROACHES

Computation is used in solving problems. Students need to develop skills in working with whole numbers and should be able to master basic facts and algorithms. To help young learners grasp the underlying concepts of addition and subtraction, they should have many opportunities to work with, group, and count objects.

Students also need to be aware that in today's world, calculators and computers are commonly used to solve problems that contain large numbers or involve complex operations. Adults use calculators and computers in their everyday work, and students need to become familiar with the various mathematical functions that calculators and computers can perform.

As students work with calculators to solve problems with lengthy and complex calculations, they need to learn how to use estimation to determine the reasonableness of their answers to problems. It is easy to put a decimal point in the wrong place or to omit a zero when entering a number in a calculator. Estimating the answer prevents students from making an error based on faulty data entry.

Students should learn techniques for solving problems mentally as well as with a paper and pencil. They also need to learn thinking strategies, such as recognizing that since 50¢ plus 50¢ makes one dollar, then 51¢ plus 58¢ would be $1.09.

RESOURCES

These resources may help teachers and parents provide a rich mathematical environment for children. The titles under "Books" provide background reading and understanding. The books listed under "Other Resources" are primarily for student use and often contain reproducible pages. This section also lists games, manipulatives, videos, sets of materials, and computer programs. There are brief descriptions of each product. Although a supplier is listed, books may also be available directly from publishers, and books and other materials may be available from several distributors.

Although efforts were made to be thorough, this resource list is not exhaustive. There are other companies that carry many fine products. In addition, new products are constantly coming on the market, and some of the items that are included may go out of print or be discontinued in the future.

This resource list, however, provides a range of available resources for teaching whole number computation.

Addresses of publishers and suppliers are listed in chapter 15.

Books

** Coburn, Terrence. **How to Teach Mathematics Using a Calculator**. Reston, Va.: National Council of Teachers of Mathematics, 1987. 58p. Also available from Dale Seymour Publications.
    This book provides exercises for individual practice, two-person games, and small-group work and includes teaching notes and answers.

** Forsten, Char. **Using Calculators Is Easy: A Step-by-Step Guide for the Classroom**. Jefferson City, Mo.: Scholastic Professional Books, 1992. 80p.

Kaye, Peggy. **Games for Math**. New York: Pantheon Books, 1987. 236p.
    Included in the book are games involving counting, addition, subtraction, multiplication, and division.

Kelleher, Heather J. **Mathworks Book B**. Boston: Houghton Mifflin, 1992. 400p.
    Topics and themes involve place value and two-digit calculations.

Taylor, Hope. **Multiplication Bike Race: Hands-on Learning Game and Thematic Units, Grades 2-5**. Jefferson City, Mo.: Scholastic Professional Books, 1992. 36p.

Other Resources

(manipulatives, games, sets, reproducibles, videos, and computer diskettes)

Calculate! Problem Solving with Calculators. Worth, Ill.: Creative Publications. By Terence Coburn. 96p. Grades 3-6.

This is a basic introduction to a calculator's features. It deals with whole-number operations and contains reproducibles.

Calculator Lotto. Rowley, Mass.: Didax Educational Resources.

The game comes with four number base cards, 42 calculator cards, and colored counters. One or more calculators are needed to play the game, but calculators are not included.

** Calculators. Worth, Ill.: Creative Publications.

Many calculators with various features and prices are available from this supplier, including *TI 108, TI MathMate Calculator, TI Math Explorer, Casio FX-300V, TI 1795 Calculator*, and *Sharp EL-243 Calculator*. Also available is *Keystrokes*, by Robert Reys, Barbara Bestgen, Terence Coburn, et al., which provides activities to clarify the best use of calculators. These books include *Counting and Place Value*, Grades 2-3, 64p.; *Addition and Subtraction*, Grades 3-6, 88p.; *Multiplication and Division*, Grades 4-6, 88p.; and *Exploring New Topics*, Grades 2-8, 64p. Materials are also sold as a set.

** Calculators. Palo Alto, Calif.: Dale Seymour Publications.

Many calculators with different features and prices are available from this supplier, including *Casio MS-70; Casio SL-450*, which comes with an activity book and blackline masters; *Casio-450 OH; Casio HS-10; Casio SL-300*; and *Sharp EL-376*. These are 100-percent solar powered and are sold individually or as sets. The company will bid on volume orders. Also available is *Calculators in Mathematics Education*, James T. Fey, editor (Reston, Va.: National Council of Teachers of Mathematics, 1992), all grades, 256p., which explores the role of calculators in the classroom. *Texas Instruments Calculator Kits* are packaged as ten calculators or as a classroom set of 30 calculators. Classroom sets include instructional materials, blackline transparency masters, and a poster. *TI-108*, Grades K-4, is a simple calculator that is available singly or in classroom sets. It also comes as *The Educator Basic Overhead Calculator* and has a keyboard layout that matches the TI-108. *The Essential TI-108 Activity Book*, by David E. Williams (Sunnyvale, Calif.: Stokes Publishing, 1993), 104p., Grades 3-9, suggests ways to integrate calculators into the classroom and includes student activity sheets. *TI MathMate* is especially designed for young learners and is available singly or in a teacher's kit of ten. To match this keyboard layout there is *The Educator Elementary Overhead Calculator*.

Cluebusters. Palo Alto, Calif.: Dale Seymour Publications. By Jean E. Haack. 64p. Grades 3-6.

This publication contains 44 math puzzles with clues to assist the player in discovering a secret word or phrase. Gives practice in addition, subtraction, multiplication, and division, and includes reproducible pages.

** = Highly recommended.   = **Computer resources.**   = **Videos.**

Cooperative Problem Solving with Calculators. Worth, Ill.: Creative Publications. By Judy Goodnow, Shirley Hoogenboom, and Ann Roper. Grades 4-6.

Activities encourage students to use calculators in problem solving. This is also available in a Spanish version, *Resolver Problems en Cooperacion con Calculadores*. Either version can also be purchased as a *Class Set* with eight calculators.

Dominoes. Columbus, Ohio: Judy/Instructo.

Addition Dominoes Set provides practice in adding sums from zero to ten and 11 to 18. *Subtraction Dominoes Set* reinforces subtracting minuends of ten or less and minuends of 11 to 18. *Multiplication Dominoes Set* reinforces multiplication facts and principles. *Division Dominoes Set* provides practice in division using three sets of dominoes.

Facts of Math: Addition. Palo Alto, Calif.: Dale Seymour Publications. By Tamara Busch and Bonnie Stoops. 96p. Grades 1-3.

This book includes teaching suggestions, reproducible work sheets, and games to help students make sense of and practice the 100 basic addition facts.

FIT for Mathematics. Rowley, Mass.: Didax Educational Resources. Developed by Swiss educators.

The program consists of heavy-duty laminated cardholders and six sets of cards with problems. When a student inserts a card in the holder, the first problem is shown. By pulling the card up farther, the answer is displayed. Subjects covered in the set include addition, subtraction, multiplication, division, fractions, metric measure and weights, and the concepts of more than and less than and of telling time.

Five in a Row Software: Mental Math. Pacific Grove, Calif.: Critical Thinking Press & Software. Grade 2 to adult.

These games require students to add, subtract, multiply, or divide numbers. Two students take turns covering numbers on a grid on the computer screen. The winner is the first to cover five numbers in a row. Available for Windows and Macintosh.

The Funshine Kids "Great Math Adventures." Birmingham, Ala.: The Re-Print Corporation. Grades 2-8.

This set of 12 40-minute videos comes with blackline masters and a teacher's guide. Each video introduces and reinforces specific math skills in addition, subtraction, multiplication, and division. The videos are available separately, as a set of six, and as a set of 12. Titles include *Sum Thing from Beyond, The Hour of Horrors—Trapped by the Evil Eye, Space Strangers, The Fatal Clue, The Mathemagician, The Case of the Missing Addends, The Invisible Caller, The Crying Hermit of Haven's Hill, The Mystery of the Old Barn, The Case of the Missing Clown, The Divided Skull,* and *Dog Gone.*

The Mad Minute. Reading, Mass.: Addison-Wesley. By Paul Shoecraft and Terry Clukey. 252p. Grades 3-8.

By using reproducible work sheets, students gain practice in basic number facts. Divided by grade level.

Mark and Re-Mark Cards. Columbus, Ohio: Judy/Instructo.

These packages of ten identical, durable 8½-inch-by-11-inch practice cards wipe clean and can be reused. Unfinished problems are on one side, and answers are on the other. Available for addition, subtraction, multiplication, division, money, and telling time.

** **Math by All Means. Multiplication: Grades 3-4**. Sausalito, Calif.: Math Solutions
Publications, 1991. By Marilyn Burns. Distributed by Cuisenaire Company of
America.

This book provides materials to help students learn multiplication through a variety
of perspectives, including geometric and numerical, and by investigating real-life
situations. *Division: Grades 3-4*, by Susan Ohanian and Marilyn Burns, uses manipulatives, posters, and three children's books, *The Doorbell Rang, 17 Kings and 42
Elephants*, and *One Hundred Hungry Ants*, to develop an understanding of division.

Math Card Games. Birmingham, Ala.: The Re-Print Corporation.

The card games *Thinkfast, Capture the Flag*, and *Gotcha!* give practice in using
addition, subtraction, multiplication, and division.

Math Magic. Tuscon, Ariz.: MindPlay. Computer diskettes for Apple II, II Plus,
IIe, IIc IIgs. Grades PreK-4. Available from NASCO.

This computer program gives students practice in counting objects and in
adding and subtracting numbers.

Math Puzzles. Rowley, Mass.: Didax Educational Resources.

Each puzzle box contains three 40-piece puzzles with an addition, subtraction,
or multiplication problem on the back of each piece and three puzzle boards.
Students must solve problems, find the answer on the puzzle board, and cover it
with puzzle pieces. Available for *Addition/Subtraction to 20; Addition/Subtraction to
100; Multiplication to 100*; and *Addition to 1,000*.

Math Word Problems: Whole Numbers. Pacific Grove, Calif.: Critical Thinking
Press & Software. By Anita Harnadek. Grade 3-adult.

This book contains word problems using whole numbers. Reproducible pages
are included.

Mathematics Laboratory, 2A. Blacklick, Ohio: SRA/McGraw Hill. Don H. Parker,
consultant; Paul Trafton and Judith Zawajewski, collaborators. Grade 4.

This kit contains skill cards, answer cards, pretests, post-tests, placement tests,
activity cards, project cards, take-home projects, mental-arithmetic problem cards,
student-record folders, a wall chart, an instruction book, and a teacher's guide.

Number Juggler. Rowley, Mass.: Didax Educational Resources.

This balance helps teach simple addition and subtraction. The juggler is
6¾-inches tall and comes with 18 number weights and two bucket weights for
playing the game. Instructions are included.

Schoolhouse Mathematics Series. Blacklick, Ohio: SRA/McGraw Hill. Includes *Mathematics 1*, Grades 1-2; *Mathematics 2*, Grades 2-3; *Mathematics 3*, Grades 3-4.

Each lab contains 400 skill cards, ten plastic overlays, ten markers, a student
record card, and a teacher's guide. Mathematics 2 and 3 also include plastic rulers.

Solar-Powered Calculator/Cash Register. Boulder, Colo.: PlayFair Toys.

Young children can play store with a working cash register and life-size play
money. Oversize buttons and a big number display make it easy to learn basic
calculator skills.

Speedway Math. Minneapolis, Minn.: MECC/Softkey International. Computer
diskette for Apple II, II Plus, IIe, IIc, IIgs. Grades 1-6. Also available from
NASCO.

This computer game provides practice in addition, subtraction, multiplication, and division.

** **Stickybear Math**. Hilton Head, S.C.: Optimum Resource. Computer diskettes for Apple II, II Plus, IIe, IIc, IIgs. Grades 1-3. Available from NASCO.

Students learn to add and subtract two-, three-, and four-digit numbers while they help Stickybear on his adventures. *Stickybear Math 2*, Grade 2 and up, concentrates on multiplication and division problems. *Stickybear Word Problems*, Grade 2 and up, offers hundreds of word problems that require the use of basic math skills.

Stickybear's Math Town. Hilton Head, S.C.: Optimum Resource. Computer diskette for Macintosh. Grades 1-5. Available from NASCO.

Six levels of difficulty provide practice in addition, subtraction, multiplication, division, and word problems. Skills are covered in English and Spanish.

Super Snake. Rowley, Mass.: Didax Educational Resources.

This game's four mathematical operations use numbers up to 50. Up to four students may play. Set includes a game board and playing pieces.

Target Practice. Palo Alto, Calif.: Dale Seymour Publications. By Margo Seymour and Dale Seymour. Grades 1-12.

Two puzzle books require students to combine given numbers using addition, subtraction, multiplication, and sometimes division to get a target number. Pages are reproducible, and answers are provided.

Teacher's Using Piaget's Theory Videotapes. By Constance Kamii. Grades 2-4. Available from Creative Publications.

Three tapes, each about 20 minutes in length, show students how to solve problems using their intuitive knowledge of numbers. Available are *Double-Column Addition, Multiplication of Two-Digit Numbers*, and *Multidigit Division*. Also available are two books by Constance Kamii: *Young Children Reinvent Arithmetic*, 283 p., shows how first-grade students create their own approaches to computation; and *Young Children Continue to Reinvent Arithmetic*, 217 p., challenges second graders to rethink math concepts.

** **Tops Calculator Problem Decks**. Palo Alto, Calif.: Dale Seymour Publications. By Carole Greenes, George Immerzeel, Linda Schulman, and Rika Spungin. Grades 3-6.

These problems are based on real-world data and situations and help students develop expertise and judgment in using calculators. Each deck contains 200 illustrated calculator cards at two levels of difficulty.

24 Games. Available from Dale Seymour and other distributors.

These games help improve mental arithmetic. Students create equations that equal 24 using the numbers on game cards. *The 24 Game*, Grade 4 to adult; *Add/Subtract Edition*, Grades 1-3; and *Multiply/Divide Edition*, Grade 3 to adult are all available.

Visual Math. Carson, Calif.: Educational Insights. 24p. Available from Dale Seymour Publications.

A set contains manipulatives and an activity book with reproducibles. The ten manipulatives give students a feel for addition and subtraction facts using numbers one through ten.

CHAPTER 9
GEOMETRY AND SPATIAL SENSE

In grades K-4, the mathematics curriculum should include two- and three-dimensional geometry so that students can:

> describe, model, draw, and classify shapes;

> investigate and predict the results of combining, subdividing, and changing shapes;

> develop spatial sense;

> relate geometric ideas to number and measurement ideas;

> recognize and appreciate geometry in their world.

from *Curriculum and Evaluation Standards for School Mathematics*, National Council of Teachers of Mathematics, 1989.

APPROACHES

Some children have a strong spatial sense at an early age. This assists them in learning about other number and measurement ideas. Students also learn about the properties of shapes by exploring with building blocks, pattern blocks, geoboards, graph papers, and other materials. A generous supply of these materials is necessary in each classroom. When they are ready, students also benefit from folding paper cutouts and using mirrors to study symmetry.

Many children seem to enjoy working with geometric shapes and may initially find more success here than in working on numerical skills.

Students need experience in combining parts into different shapes, in predicting, for example, what will happen when a shape is rotated or when the length of a side is changed. Such practice should be encouraged because geometric skills are often essential to problem solving in which the student needs to make a drawing or diagram to find the answer to a question.

While working with shapes, students will also increase their mathematical vocabulary to include such words as *right angles*, *squares*, *above*, *below*, and *behind*. This vocabulary development should come about naturally as students work with shapes in simple activities.

RESOURCES

These resources may help teachers and parents provide a rich mathematical environment for children. The titles under "Books" provide background reading and understanding. The books listed under "Other Resources" are primarily for student use and often contain reproducible pages. This section also lists games, manipulatives, videos, sets of materials, and computer programs. There are brief descriptions of each product. Although a supplier is listed, books may also be available directly from publishers, and books and other materials may be available from several distributors.

Although efforts were made to be thorough, this resource list is not exhaustive. There are other companies that carry many fine products. In addition, new products are constantly coming on the market, and some of the items that are included may go out of print or be discontinued in the future.

This resource list, however provides a range of available resources for teaching geometry and spatial sense.

Addresses of publishers and suppliers are listed in chapter 15.

Books

** Burk, Donna, Allyn Snider, and Paula Symonds. **Math Excursions Series, K, 1, 2**. Portsmouth, N.H.: Heinemann, 1992. *Grade K*, 266p.; *Grade 1*, 259p.; *Grade 2*, 218p.

** Burns, Marilyn. "The Shapes of Math." Part 2 of **Math for Smarty Pants**. Boston: Little, Brown, 1982. 128p.

Forte, Imogene, and Joy MacKenzie. **Creative Math Experiences**. Nashville, Tenn.: Incentive Publications, 1983. 176p. Grades K-3.
This book contains information on shapes, size words, and counting by sets.

Ross, Catherine Sheldrick. **Circles: Fun Ideas for Getting Around in Math**. Reading, Mass.: Addison Wesley Longman, 1993. 80p.

Van de Walle, John A. **Elementary School Mathematics: Teaching Developmentally**. 2d ed. White Plains, N.Y.: Longman, 1994. 544p.
Chapter 17 is especially helpful in working with geometry.

Wilson, Jeni, and Lynda Cutting. **It's Time: Celebrating Maths with Projects**. Portsmouth, N.Y.: Heinemann, 1993. 112p.

Other Resources

(manipulatives, games, sets, reproducibles, videos, and computer diskettes)

Angle Study Dominoes. Rowley, Mass.: Didax Educational Resources.

The set of 24 dominoes gives students practice in visual recognition of angle measures as they match angle values with the pictorial depictions. The set comes with instructions.

Archiblocks. Vergennes, Vt.: Interactive Arts. All ages. Also available from Dale Seymour Publications.

Various sets of wooden blocks allow students to learn about geometry and relationships through architecture. Available kits include *Roman, Egyptian, Gothic, Greek, Islamic, Post Modern*, and *Renaissance*. Each kit contains 50 wooden pieces and a poster.

** Chalkboard Pieces. Worth, Ill.: Creative Publications.

Included are *Chalkboard Rule; Chalkboard Compass; Chalkboard Protractor;* and the *Chalkboard Geometry Set*, which includes all three of the above.

D.I.M.E. Geometry. Buffalo, N.Y.: SI Manufacturing Limited.

This program in three-dimensional geometry was developed by Geoff Giles and is geared to developing geometric principles in spatial awareness and isometric drawings. The set contains solids of geometric shapes, a teacher's guide, and three books.

D-Stix. Available from Creative Publications.

These are color-coded plastic rods and multipronged connectors with instruction sheets. Available are the *Junior Kit* with 220 pieces, the *Apprentice Kit* with 370 pieces, and the *Engineering Kit* with 464 pieces.

From Crystals to Kites. Palo Alto, Calif.: Dale Seymour Publications. By Ron Kremer. 96p. Grades 4-8.

Students build three-dimensional structures in solid geometry units. Comes with teacher's notes, blackline masters, and patterns.

** Gaining Spatial Sense with Pattern Blocks. Rowley, Mass.: Didax Educational Resources. By Don Balka. 54p. Grades 2-4.

This book of pattern-block activities helps students learn about geometric shapes. Also available are sets of 250 *Pattern Blocks—Wooden*. Each set of one-centimeter thick blocks contains 25 yellow hexagons, 25 orange squares, 50 green triangles, 50 red trapezoids, 50 blue parallelograms, and 50 tan rhombuses.

Geo Strips. Rowley, Mass.: Didax Educational Resources.

The set consists of 68 rods of various sizes, a box of connectors, a protractor, and a set of 11 graded work cards. Students fasten the strips into a variety of plane geometric figures.

** Geoblocks. Worth, Ill.: Creative Publications. Grades K-8.

The set contains 336 metric ESS Geoblocks, including 180 cubes, 42 rectangular prisms, 108 triangular prisms, and six pyramids cut from hardwood in a variety of sizes. *Geoblocks Jobcards*, by Micaelia Randolph Brummett and Linda Holden Charles, are sets of 23 cards and include *Exploring, Which Block? Build This! Constructions, Puzzles,* and *Jackets*. These are also available as a *Series* and as a *Complete Kit*, which contains the six Jobcards sets and 336 Geoblocks.

** Geoblocks. Rowley, Mass.: Didax Educational Resources.

A set of 330 geoblocks includes 180 cubes, 42 rectangular prisms, 102 triangular prisms, and six pyramids. These are made of hardwood and come with a teacher's guide.

** Geoboards. Worth, Ill.: Creative Publications.

Geoboards allow students to stretch rubber bands around pegs to represent mathematical concepts such as shapes and angles. The *5 x 5 Pin Geoboards* are available in 12-inch and six-inch sizes and are sold individually and in sets of ten. The *Bucket of 5 x 5 Geoboards* comes in a set of 11. Also available are the *Geoboards Sampler*, which includes 16 5-by-5 Geoboards, rubber bands, and a 16-page *Take off with Geoboards* booklet; *5 x 5 Pin Geoboard for the Overhead Projector*; the eight-inch-by-eight-inch *Heavy Duty Deluxe Geoboards*, which are sold individually and in sets of 13; and ten-inch-by-ten-inch *Geoboards*, which come in sets of five and 30; *Rubber Bands*; *Primary Jobcards: Puzzles with Geoboards*, Grades PreK-2, by Ann Roper, comes as a set of 21 cards and is also available as a *Starter Set* with materials for 22 students.

** Geoboards. Palo Alto, Calif.: Dale Seymour Publications.

Eight-inch and Ten-inch Geoboards are available in wood, colored plastic, and transparent plastic. *Large Geoboards* are opaque with 121 pegs in a square formation on one side and 137 pegs in a pentagon formation on the other side. These are also available in clear plastic for overhead projection. *Circular Geoboards* are available individually, in sets of five, and as templates. These are also available in transparent plastic for overhead projection. *Geoboard Teacher's Manual*, by John Bradford, 48p., Grades K-12, contains reproducible activities. *Dot Paper Geometry—With or Without a Geoboard*, by Charles Lund, 82p., Grades 4-8, contains 62 reproducible sheets for activities. *Link-a-Board* is an expandable geoboard with a special linking feature that allows students to connect four clear geoboards. A teacher's guide is included.

** Geoboards. Rowley, Mass.: Didax Educational Resources.

Wooden geoboards are available individually, in sets, and in various sizes. Also available are *Centimeter Geoboard—Plastic*; *Double Sided Pin Geoboard—Plastic*; *Shapes Geoboard—Plastic*; *Double Sided 6 x 6 Pin Geoboard—Plastic*; and a *Transparent Geoboard* for use with an overhead projector.

✱✱ **Geoboards**. Columbus, Ohio: Judy/Instructo.

Six double-sided, plastic geoboards are included with a five-inch square pin-to-pin grid of 25 on one side and a circular arrangement of 17 pegs on the other. Geoboards come in six colors with rubber bands. Also available are a *Beginning Geoboard Set*, which includes 15 activity cards, and a transparent *Overhead Geoboard*.

✱✱ **Geoboards**. Buffalo, N.Y.: SI Manufacturing Limited.

These are available in a variety of sizes, with different numbers of pegs, including clear boards for use with an overhead projector. A teacher's guide is included.

Geo-Fix Solid Geometry Construction Set. Rowley, Mass.: Didax Educational Resources. Grades 3-6.

These heavy card-stock pieces fit together with tabs and slots to form a durable structure. The set contains 90 triangles, 30 squares, 15 pentagons, and 15 hexagons.

Geometric Building Set. Boulder, Colo.: PlayFair Toys.

This set contains 52 plastic pieces in ten geometric shapes. Pieces have unique ribs and can fit together to build such things as cars and houses.

Geometric Models. Palo Alto, Calif.: Dale Seymour Publications.

These models are available as a wooden set of 12 pieces, which range in size from two inches to three inches, and as a plastic set of 30 pieces, with sizes from two inches to 4½ inches.

Geometric Models. Rowley, Mass.: Didax Educational Resources.

These three-dimensional models come in a storage tray and are made of molded plastic. They come in sets of 30 or 15 shapes.

Geometric Solids Sampler. Worth, Ill.: Creative Publications. Grades K-6.

This sampler includes a 16-page booklet, *Take Off! With Geometric Solids*, and four sets of geometric solids. The *Wooden Geometric Solids, Basic Set* is made up of 12 precision-cut hardwood pieces; the *Simple Set* contains six pieces; the *Complete Set*, 18 pieces; *Geometry Jobcards: Geometric Solids*, Grades 5-8, is a set of 22 activity cards.

Geometry and Spatial Sense. Reston, Va.: National Council of Teachers of Mathematics, 1993. By John Del Grande and Lorna Morrow. 64p. Grades K-6. Also available from Dale Seymour Publications.

This book helps students to develop spatial perception, geometry language, and concepts. Comes with notes, references, and reproducible materials.

Geometry Dominoes. Rowley, Mass.: Didax Educational Resources.

These 24 dominoes are printed on heavy plastic and help teach recognition of two- and three-dimensional shapes.

Geometry Resource Kit. Rowley, Mass.: Didax Educational Resources. Teacher's guide by Don Balka. Grades 4-8.

The kit includes *Geometric Models, Geo-Fix, Solid Geometry Construction Set, Plane Geometry Stamps, Three-Dimensional Geometric Stamps, Angle Study Dominoes, Name and Shape Dominoes, Geometry Dominoes, Geo Strips*, and *PlasTek Geometrical Shapes Templates*.

Geometry Stamps, Plane and **Three-Dimensional**. Rowley, Mass.: Didax Educational Resources.

The 15 stamps in the plane geometry set come in an assortment of regular and irregular plane shapes that produce clear imprints. There are 14 stamps in the three-dimensional geometric stamps. They show the shape of each design and use dotted lines to illustrate its three-dimensional construction.

The Geometry Template. White Plains, N.Y.: Cuisenaire Company of America. Grades 4-12.

This plastic template shows 32 geometric shapes and has prepunched holes for three-ring-binder storage.

Geometry Templates. Worth, Ill.: Creative Publications. Grades 3-10.

These templates are 8½ inches by 11 inches, and the set of two offers a total of 64 polygons. Templates are prepunched for three-ring-binder storage.

Geometry Tools. Worth, Ill.: Creative Publications.

Among the materials available for teaching geometric concepts are *Circle Perfect Compass, Circle Protractor, Protractor, Plastic Center Locator, Circle Perfect Compass Stylus Replacement, Geometric Shapes Tracers, Triman Classmate Compass, Triman Compass for the Overhead Projector, Super Triman Compass, Safe-T Protractor, Safe-T Chalkboard Protractor, Safe-T Student Compass, Safe-T Overhead Compass,* and *Safe-T Chalkboard Compass.*

Geometry Tools. Birmingham, Ala.: The Re-Print Corporation.

Among the materials available for teaching geometric concepts are *Geometric Plastic Forms,* which include a cone, a cube, a sphere, a hemisphere, an ellipsoid, two cylinders, three pyramids, four prisms, and an instruction booklet; *Pentominoes* and *Pattern Cards; Wooden Geometric Solids,* with pieces ranging in size from two inches to three inches; *Pin Geoboards* in various sizes; *Pin Circle Geoboards; Geoboards for the Overhead Projector; Mathcards for the Geoboard,* Grades 1-6; *Puzzlers for Overhead Geoboards,* Grades 1-4; *Geoboard Activity Sheets;* and *Chalkboard Drawing Instruments,* including a straightedge, triangle, protractor, and T-square.

Geominoes. Rowley, Mass.: Didax Educational Resources.

The set contains 42 laminated puzzle cards and stimulates students to make connections and develop spatial sense. Cards are available with straightedge or swirl designs. When arranged, they form a seven-card by six-card array.

GeoMirror. Worth, Ill.: Creative Publications. Grades 3-12.

The reflective mirror and drawing tool are available individually or in a set of 32. *Mira Math Resource Book,* Grades 4-6, contains activities using the GeoMirror to view, move, and draw images.

Giant Geometric Shapes Floor Tiles. Rowley, Mass.: Didax Educational Resources.

There are four colors of each shape. The square is 13 inches by 13 inches; the rectangle is 12 inches by ten inches; the circle is 13 inches in diameter; the triangle has 12½-inch sides. Tiles are made of polyester carpet with nonslip rubber backing. A teacher's guide is included.

Giant Inset Shapes. Rowley, Mass.: Didax Educational Resources.

These shapes are made of polyester carpet with nonslip rubber backing. The set includes six giant shapes (square, rectangle, circle, triangle, pentagon, and hexagon) and each shape is made of five pieces in sizes ranging from 1½ inches to 12½ inches.

Googolplex. Worth, Ill.: Creative Publications. Grades K-12.

These construction pieces snap together with connectors, rods, wheels, and axles. The teacher's guide includes directions for various activities.

** Hands-on Geoboards. Worth, Ill.: Creative Publications.

This is a reproducible, 144-page binder of problem-solving activities for five-by-five-pin geoboards. It's also available as a *Starter Set*, with enough materials for 12 students; and as a *Classroom Set*, with enough materials for 30 students. *Moving on with Geoboards*, by Shirley Hoogenboom, Grades 4-6, is a 128-page binder with 112 activities for five-by-five pin geoboard activities. *Moving on with Geoboards Starter Set* includes a binder and materials for up to 22 students. *20 Thinking Questions for Geoboards: Grades 3-6*, by Kathryn Walker and Kelly Stewart, 112p., contains activities for five-by-five pin geoboards. *20 Thinking Questions for Geoboards Class Set: Grades 3-6* contains a book, 16 circle and five-by-five pin geoboards, one each of circle and five-by-five pin geoboard for the overhead projector, and rubber bands.

Large 3D Shapes. Rowley, Mass.: Didax Educational Resources.

Nine large, plastic geometric shapes allow students to observe relationships among area, volume, shape, form, size, and pattern. An instruction guide is included in the kit.

Math by All Means. Sausalito, Calif.: Math Solutions Publications, 1994. Distributed by Cuisenaire Company of America.

Geometry: Grades 1-2 by Chris Confer. This unit helps children develop an understanding of the properties of shape. *Geometry: Grades 3-4*, by Cheryl Rectanus, is designed as a five-week lesson in sorting, classifying, drawing, describing, combining, and modeling shapes.

Math Kit, K-1. Columbus, Ohio: Judy/Instructo.

Kit contains mirrors, graphing mat, one set of attribute desk blocks, one numberite, five blank dice, five clear spinners, 30 felt numbers, 300 counters, 250 plastic pattern blocks, 500 rainbow links, 102 rainbow math cubes, six geoboards, 240 linking cubes, two sets of student overhead tangrams, overhead-project materials, and storage buckets.

Math Manipulatives. Blacklick, Ohio: SRA/McGraw Hill.

Among items available are *Shape Sorting Box; Shape Templates; Clear Stencils; Multi Cubes; Shape Stamps; Multi Cube Number Track; Tangram and Puzzle Cards; Pegs/Pegboards; Color Cubes; Parquetry; Small Parquetry Designs I, II, III.*

Mira Math Kit. Grades 4-6. Available from Dale Seymour Publications.

Available are a plastic Mira and a Mira Book. The Mira is a transparent plastic tool that helps students observe geometric figures and understand their properties. The activities in the book involve simple perception, using paper and pencil, rulers, compasses, and more.

Name the Shape Dominoes. Rowley, Mass.: Didax Educational Resources.

This 24-domino set is printed on heavy plastic and helps teach names of various geometric shapes. Instructions are included.

Notes on a Triangle. Palo Alto, Calif.: Dale Seymour Publications. 80p. All grades. Also available from Cuisenaire Company of America.

Kit contains a video, book, poster, and manipulative set. The video shows a triangle dividing into many complex designs. The manipulatives allow students to explore the video's underlying concepts and principles.

Oxford Level. Rowley, Mass.: Didax Educational Resources.

Use of the level introduces beginning geometry concepts. It measures the angle of any surface with an accuracy of one-half degree. Teacher's notes are included.

** **Pattern Blocks**. Buffalo, N.Y.: SI Manufacturing Limited.

Solid and hollow pattern blocks and pattern blocks for overhead projectors are available in six shapes and colors, along with teacher's guides.

** **Pattern Blocks**. Richardson, Tex.: Kaidy Educational Resources.

Available are overhead pattern blocks; a pattern-block template to fashion your own set of pattern blocks; and a 170-page book, *Let's Pattern Block It*, by Peggy McLean, Lee Jenkins, and Jack McLaughlin, for exploring shapes, sizes, congruence, patterns, angles, and fractions.

Pentominoes. Worth, Ill.: Creative Publications.

Sets contain 12 pieces and are available as a single set or as a bucket of eight sets. Also available are *Pentominoes for the Overhead Projector. Hands-on Pentominoes*, Grades K-3, is a 144-page binder with single-page activities to aid students' understanding of geometric shapes and relationships. A *Hands-on Pentominoes Starter Set* includes the binder above and six sets of Pentominoes, and a *Pentominoes Intermediate Starter Set* includes six sets of Pentominoes plus a book. These are also available separately, as is *Pentomino Activities, Lessons and Puzzles*, Grades 3-8, by Henri Picciotto.

Pentominoes. Columbus, Ohio: Judy/Instructo. Grade 1 and up.

Available as a 12-piece set, as overheads, and packages of 12 sets. Each plastic 12-piece set fits together to form a six-inch-by-ten-inch rectangle.

Pentominoes and Tangrams. Buffalo, N.Y.: SI Manufacturing Limited.

These are available in a variety of sets with teacher's guides. These can be used to develop a sense of spatial relationships and to improve students' problem-solving skills.

Pholdit. Hayward, Calif.: Activity Resources Company, 1972. By Steve Goldberg. 36p. Grade 2 and up. Also available from NASCO.

This book includes step-by-step directions for making a pyramid, chrysler star, crystal, and 24-pointed star. Materials needed are paste, scissors, and paper.

Plas-Tek Geometrical Shapes Templates. Rowley, Mass.: Didax Educational Resources.

There are plastic templates of 18 geometrical shapes imprinted with the name of the shape. An instruction card is included. The square template is two inches by two inches.

Polydron. Santa Ana, Calif.: Polydron USA. All grades. Also available from Dale Seymour Publications.

Polydron is a three-dimensional construction set that allows students to explore properties of space and shapes as they create simple and complex geometric and abstract shapes. Available as a starter set, advanced set, combo set, a classroom kit, and with packages of individual pieces. Sets include red, yellow, green, and blue pieces. Also available is *Exploring with Polydron*, by Marilyn Komarc and Gwen Clay, for Grades 3-9. *Book 1*, 52p., provides lessons, a materials list, an overview, step-by-step instructions, and extension activities. One basic polydron set is needed to carry out the activities. *K-5 Elementary Geometry Lessons Using the Polydron System*, by Marilyn and Ernest Woodward, 104p., is also available. It contains 31 small-group activities using the polydron construction system.

Polygon Tiles. Worth, Ill.: Creative Publications. Grades 3-10.
These plastic tiles include 64 distinct shapes representing six classes of polygons.

Polyhedra Blocks. Palo Alto, Calif.: Dale Seymour Publications. All grades. Also available from Cuisenaire Company of America.
The basic kit contains 34 pieces. Also available are an introductory set, an advanced set, task cards, a teacher's book, and vinyl faces only. A magnetic process aligns related faces of these blocks, which then allows students to explore three-dimensional geometry.

Power Solids. White Plains, N.Y.: Cuisenaire Company of America. All grades.
In this set, the 12 shapes are transparent, blue three-dimensional solids ranging from one inch to two inches in height and width. A teacher's guide is included.

** **Puzzlers for Overhead Geoboards**. Birmingham, Ala.: The Re-Print Corporation. Grades 1-4.
This 15-card set challenges geoboard puzzlers using the overhead projector. A transparent five-by-five pin geoboard is necessary but not included in the set.

Shape Starship. Computer diskette for Apple II, II Plus, IIe, IIc, IIgs. Grades K-3. Available from NASCO.
This diskette provides basic readiness skills using Shape Match, Size and Shape Match, Shapes and Patterns, and Shape and Picture Match. Includes a teacher's guide.

** **Shapes and Sizes Attribute Pieces**. Worth, Ill.: Creative Publications. Grades PreK-3.
This 96-piece set contains plastic triangles, rectangles, circles, and squares. Shapes come in four colors and a variety of sizes, and the dimensions of every piece are multiples of other pieces. *20 Thinking Questions for Shapes and Sizes: Grades 1-3*, by Kathryn Walker and Kelly Stewart, 112p., contains 20 open-ended lessons. Also available with manipulatives as a *Classroom Kit* for 30 students and as a *Starter Set* for eight students.

** **Spatial Problem Solving with Cuisenaire Rods**. White Plains, N.Y.: Cuisenaire Company of America, 1984. By Patricia S. Davidson and Robert E. Willcutt. 66p. Grades 4-8.
This book contains visual explorations with Cuisenaire rods. Pages in the book can be reproduced.

Spectra Blocks. Buffalo, N.Y.: SI Manufacturing Limited.
These blocks are made of high-density polyurethane and come in four colors and 25 shapes.

** Tangrams. Columbus, Ohio: Judy/Instructo. Grades K-6.

These are available as *Tangram Combo Packs*, *Tangram Pieces*, *Overhead Tangrams*, and with two books: *Windows to Tangrams Level 1*, Grades K-3; and *Level 2*, Grades 4-6.

** Tangrams. Richardson, Tex.: Kaidy Educational Resources.

Available are tangram pieces, cards, a tangram template for making your own tangram pieces, and a 64-page book, *Tangram Games & Puzzles*, by Bill McConnell, which is filled with tangram activities.

 TesselMania. Minneapolis, Minn.: MECC/Softkey International. Computer diskette for Macintosh. Grades 3-12. Also available from NASCO.

This program takes the study of tessellations and their underlying geometric principles to a higher level. It comes with a teacher's guide and training video.

Theodolite. Rowley, Mass.: Didax Educational Resources.

This is a freestanding instrument for simple surveying and is made of heavy-duty plastic. Instructions for use are included.

3-D Geoshapes. Rowley, Mass.: Didax Educational Resources.

Sets of materials are available to teach solid geometry. They are available separately or as a classroom kit. Parts include triangles, squares, a pentagon with a triangle, a hexagon with a square, an explorations kit, a geodesic-dome construction set, and two 64-page books: *Geoshapes K-2* and *Geoshapes 3-6*. The geoshapes are of lightweight plastic and make firm connections.

Visual Thinking. Palo Alto, Calif.: Dale Seymour Publications. By Dale Seymour. *Set A*, Grades 4-10.

This 100-card set provides students with practice in spatial perception and visual discrimination.

** Wooden Geometric Solids. Columbus, Ohio: Judy/Instructo.

Included are six wooden pieces: sphere, cone, cylinder, cube, triangular prism, and pyramid.

CHAPTER 10

MEASUREMENT

In grades K-4, the mathematics curriculum should include measurement so that students can:

➤ understand the attributes of length, capacity, weight, mass, area, volume, time, temperature, and angle;

➤ develop the process of measuring and concepts related to units of measurement.

➤ make and use estimates of measurement;

➤ make and use measurements in problem and everyday situations.

from *Curriculum and Evaluation Standards for School Mathematics*,
National Council of Teachers of Mathematics, 1989.

APPROACHES

Measurement is a part of mathematics that children frequently use in everyday situations, so they need many opportunities to develop measurement skills. As simple an activity as thinking about an empty box helps students discover that they might measure its height, how much it holds, how much it weighs, or its perimeter.

Young students should experiment with many units and find out, for example, "how many erasers tall" a fellow student is or how many "paper clips wide" a piece of paper is. These early investigations of unique units of measurement ready the child for eventually measuring with rulers, centimeter sticks, thermometers, and so on.

Measurement is used naturally in other areas of the curriculum. Music and art provide rich opportunities for different types of measurement, and science activities involve measuring growth, distance, speed, temperature, liquids, and solids. Map work in social studies, figuring out the time in different time zones, and calculating longitude and latitude are other examples of cross-curricular uses of measurement.

Measurement is gradually incorporated into many aspects of problem solving and eventually becomes a valuable tool in teaching the importance of fractions and decimals.

RESOURCES

These resources may help teachers and parents provide a rich mathematical environment for children. The titles under "Books" provide background reading and understanding. The books listed under "Other Resources" are primarily for student use and often contain reproducible pages. This section also lists games, manipulatives, videos, sets of materials, and computer programs. There are brief descriptions of each product. Although a supplier is listed, books may also be available directly from publishers, and books and other materials may be available from several distributors.

Although every effort was made to be thorough, this resource list is not exhaustive. There are other companies that carry many fine products. In addition, new products are constantly coming on the market, and some of the items that are included may go out of print or be discontinued in the future.

This resource list, however, provides a range of available resources for teaching measurement.

Addresses of publishers and suppliers are listed in chapter 15.

Books

** Baker, Dave. **How Big Is the Moon? Whole Maths in Action**. Portsmouth, N.H.: Heinemann, 1990. 110p.

Burk, Donna, Allyn Snider, and Paula Symonds. **Math Excursions Series, K, 1, 2**. Portsmouth, N.H.: Heinemann, 1992. *Grade K, 266p.; Grade 1, 259p.; Grade 2, 218p.*

Burns, Marilyn. **This Book Is About Time**. Boston: Little, Brown, 1978. 128p. Grades 5-8.
This book is filled with entertaining facts and background material.

Kelleher, Heather J. **Mathworks Book B**. Boston: Houghton Mifflin, 1992. 400p.
A section on measurement is included.

Van de Walle, John A. **Elementary School Mathematics: Teaching Developmentally**. 2d ed. White Plains, N.Y.: Longman, 1994. 544p.
Chapter 16 contains information on measurement.

** Wilson, Jeni, and Lynda Cutting. **It's Time: Celebrating Maths with Projects**. Portsmouth, N.H.: Heinemann, 1993. 112p.

Other Resources

(manipulatives, games, sets, reproducibles, videos, and computer diskettes)

✱✱ All-Purpose Teaching Clock. Rowley, Mass.: Didax Educational Resources.

This clock has six different options. Its dial displays minutes, digital time, before and after the hour, roman numerals, and a blank face to write on.

✱✱ Balance Scale with Weights. Worth, Ill.: Creative Publications. Grades 4-12.

This precise balance has a beam made of die-cast aluminum. It also has a zero adjustment wheel. *Primary Balance*, Grades K-6, is a simple-to-use balance. The hoppers may be removed from the scales and used as scoops. The balance has a one-liter capacity and a one-gram sensitivity. *Easy Scale with Masses*, Grades K-6, has a fulcrum pin that allows the beam to rock freely and give accurate weight comparisons. Includes 20, five-gram plastic masses. Extra masses are available in sets of 20. *Stacking Balance*, Grades K-3, is a simple, two-piece, molded scale. *Bucket and Pan Balance*, Grades K-6, includes two interchangeable buckets and pans, sliding weights for zero adjustment, and a numbered track beam. Also available are *Three Bear Counters* in three sizes and four colors weighing four, eight, and 12 grams and ranging in height from one inch to 1½ inches. *Plastic Stacking Masses*, a 40-piece set, includes ten five-gram, five ten-gram, five 20-gram, and 20 one-gram stackable masses.

Big Teaching Clock. Rowley, Mass.: Didax Educational Resources.

This clock is 15¾ inches across and has raised numbers and markings.

Bucket Balance. Rowley, Mass.: Didax Educational Resources.

The arms of this balance hold 2½-quart buckets. It measures 18 inches by 12½ inches across and is made of plastic. Available separately are the color-coded *Plastic Stacking Weights*, which include 20 orange one-gram weights, ten blue two-gram weights, four red five-gram weights, two green ten-gram weights, and one yellow 20-gram weight.

Bulletin Board Set. Greensboro, N.C.: Carson-Dellosa Publishing.

The *Measurement Bulletin Board* set includes five 17-inch-by-22-inch charts with standards and metric measurement for temperature, time, capacity, length, weight, and mass. Also comes with a resource guide.

Capacity Measures. Rowley, Mass.: Didax Educational Resources.

This set contains measures to hold $125cm^3$, $250cm^3$, $500cm^3$, and $1000cm^3$.

✱✱ Chalkboard Tools. Palo Alto, Calif.: Dale Seymour Publications.

Math Set includes three chalkboard tools: protractor, compass, and straightedge. Available in wood or plastic, as a set, or separately. A variety of student rulers, yardsticks, and protractors are also available.

Clinometer. Rowley, Mass.: Didax Educational Resources.

Students point the clinometer at the top of a tree or building they are measuring, pull the trigger, wait for the disc to stop spinning, and then read the angle on the protractor. They can then calculate height by using the formula found in the guide included with the set.

✱✱ = Highly recommended. ⌸ **= Computer resources.** **= Videos.**

Clock Dominoes. Fort Atkinson, Wis.: NASCO.

This game includes 45 dominoes. It may be played covering hours, half hours, and quarter hours, using clockfaces, digital time, and written time.

Clock Face Stamp. Rowley, Mass.: Didax Educational Resources.

This stamp produces 2⅝-inch impressions of clock faces. Also available as a 3-inch-by-3¾-inch *Dual Clock Face Rubber Stamp* with digital and analog time.

Clockworks. Minneapolis, Minn.: MECC/Softkey International. Computer Diskettes for Apple II, II Plus, IIe, IIc, IIgs. Grades 1-3. Also available from NASCO.

The selection of Arabic or Roman clock faces has multiple difficulty levels for teaching students about clocks and telling time.

** **Clockworks Geared Demonstration Clock**. Worth, Ill.: Creative Publications. Grades PreK-3.

This plastic clock comes with a stand and measures 14 inches by 14 inches. A blue minute hand matches the minutes indicated on the clock face while a magenta hour hand matches the hour numbers. The movements of the hands are linked with built-in gears. Also available is a plastic *Clockworks Geared Student Clock*, which measures five inches by five inches, and *Clockworks Student Clocks* in sets of ten. *Buckets of Pupil Clock Dials* made of cardboard are also available in sets of 30. *Student Clock Faces* printed in black-and-white plastic are available in sets of ten or 30. *Clock Faces for the Overhead Project* are available in sets of five.

Discover Time. Big Spring, Tex.: Gamco. Computer diskette for Macintosh. Grades K-5. Available from NASCO.

Students play pirates looking for buried treasure and make progress in their search by answering questions about telling time.

Exploring and Observing Weather Kit. Columbus, Ohio: Judy/Instructo.

The kit comes with weather equipment, reproducible activity sheets, and a book, *Weather Watch*, which ties weather to mathematics and other curricular areas.

Getting into Area. Palo Alto, Calif.: Dale Seymour Publications. By Anne M. Bloomer. 74p. Grades 3-6.

This book includes background on learning geometry and measurement, assessment notes, rubric scoring, and blackline masters.

Grid Paper Pads and Overhead Grids. Worth, Ill.: Creative Publications.

These are tools for making graphs and charts which are sold in 50-sheet pads.

Height Measure. Rowley, Mass.: Didax Educational Resources.

This centimeter- and inch-marked height measure can be used freestanding, or it can be wall mounted.

Hexagram Weight Set. Birmingham, Ala.: The Re-Print Corporation. Grades 1-8.

In this set of 54 color-coded, stacking masses, each color represents a different thickness and mass.

Liter Set. Rowley, Mass.: Didax Educational Resources.

The containers in this set have different heights, widths, or base areas. Four hold one liter of liquids, and the fifth container is a 500-cubic-centimeter cylinder.

✻✻ **Liter Set**. Birmingham, Ala.: The Re-Print Corporation.

The set contains five clear, plastic containers graduated in 100-milliliter units. The rectangular prism, cube, and two different cylinders each holds one liter. A small cylinder holds 500 milliliters.

Math Balance. Birmingham, Ala.: The Re-Print Corporation.

Set includes balance, 20 ten-gram weights, and an instruction booklet. A set of 40 extra weights is available. Also available is *Number Juggler*. The juggler is 6¾ inches tall, and the set includes 18 number weights and two bucket weights. Instructions are included. The *Primary Rocker Balance*, Grade PreK and up, comes with transparent buckets for solid and liquid measurement.

✻✻ **Measurement Materials**. Palo Alto, Calif.: Dale Seymour Publications.

Available are *Math Balance; Spectrum School Balance; Clear Buckets; Simple Scale; Poster & Book Called Metric for Me!; Pan Balance; 5-KG Spring Scale, Platform Scale; Graduated Cup, Pint, Quart Set; Graduated Liter Box; One-Minute Timer; Metric Dry Measure Set; Metric Spoon Set; Student Thermometers; Measuring Tapes; Electronic Timer; Metric Stacking Masses; Clear Plastic Volume Set;* and *TeachTimer,* a timer, stopwatch, and clock in one.

✻✻ **Measurement Materials**. Buffalo, N.Y.: SI Manufacturing Limited.

Available are spring scales, metric dry-measure sets, metric spoon sets, graduated cylinders and beakers, liter boxes, meter sticks, rulers, metric rulers, tapes, trundle wheels, growth charts, clock faces, thermometers, and balances.

Measuring Devices. Minneapolis, Minn.: Fidelity Products Co.

The Pocket Handyman III calculator works directly in feet and inches, decimal feet and inches, fractions, yards, meters, centimeters, and millimeters. It converts to and from all dimensions. *Rolatape Measure Master* can be used to measure hard surfaces indoors and out. The three styles, Sonin 45, Sonin 60 PRO, and Sonin Combo PRO, are electronic distance-measuring tools that will work indoors or outdoors and can compute areas and volumes.

Metric Bottle Set. Birmingham, Ala.: The Re-Print Corporation. Grade K and up.

Includes five graduated plastic bottles with lids: 100, 250, 500, 1,000, and 2,000 milliliters. Also available is the *Metric Volume Set,* which contains five graduated plastic beakers in ten, 50, 100, and 1,000 milliliters. *Liquid Measure Set* is also available in gallon, quart, pint, and gill.

Metric Graduated Beakers. Worth, Ill.: Creative Publications.

Set includes one container in each of the following sizes: 50 milliliters, 100 milliliters, 250 milliliters, 600 milliliters, and 1,000 milliliters.

Metric Wall Chart. Birmingham, Ala.: The Re-Print Corporation. Grade 2 and up.

The 73-centimeter-by-106-centimeter chart helps students visualize metric length, volume, mass, area, and temperature.

"Minutes Past" and "Minutes To" Dominoes. Rowley, Mass.: Didax Educational Resources. Grades 2-3.

These two sets of dominoes illustrate the concepts of before and after the hour. Each set contains 36 plastic dominoes.

** Money Big Box. Blacklick, Ohio: SRA/McGraw Hill. Grades 2-6.

This ready-to-use math center includes coins, bills, money dominoes, puzzles, drill cards, and games.

Money Challenge. Big Spring, Tex.: Gamco. Grades 1-5. Available from NASCO.

This is a computer diskette for Macintosh. The management system keeps records for as many as 500 students. The game format for two players gives practice in working with money.

Money Kit. Columbus, Ohio: Judy/Instructo.

This money kit contains activity cards, money dominoes, the make-a-dollar card game, bills and coins for use with the overhead projector, 200 classroom bills, 228 classroom coins, and a plastic money tray. Items are also available separately.

Money Works. Minneapolis, Minn.: MECC/Softkey International. Grades 1-4.

Diskettes for Apple II, II Plus, IIe, IIc, IIgs. Also available from NASCO.

Problem-solving activities about coins and currency are featured. Comes with a teacher's guide.

The Original Judy Clock. Columbus, Ohio: Judy/Instructo. Grades PreK-3.

This 12¾-inch-by-13½-inch clock has movable hands and functioning gears and comes with a teacher's guide. Also available are hardboard *Mini-Judy Clocks*.

Overhead Thermometer. Birmingham, Ala.: The Re-Print Corporation.

This ten-inch model has an adjustable red bar that indicates temperatures from 100 degrees Celsius to 40 degrees Fahrenheit.

Rocker Scales and **One Liter Rocker Scales**. Rowley, Mass.: Didax Educational Resources. Grades K-6.

The Rocker Scales have detachable tubs on the balance with centimeter markings on the inside to measure volume. The One Liter Rocker Scales have clear buckets that hold one liter of fluid.

Rulers. Worth, Ill.: Creative Publications.

Vinyl inch and metric rulers are available in sets of 20. Fifteen-centimeter clear rulers are available in sets of 12 or 144. Hardwood meter rulers are graduated on one side in millimeter units and on the other in ⅛-inch units and are sold in sets of six. Double-sided measuring tapes are 60-inch plastic tapes with inch scales on one side; centimeters and millimeters are on the reverse.

Rulers. Birmingham, Ala.: The Re-Print Corporation.

Plastic student rulers are available in packages of ten, with a 20-centimeter scale on one side and a 200-millimeter scale on the other. Also available is a demonstration meter stick with a color-coded side; a measuring tape marked off from zero to 150 centimeters; and a tape that retracts into a plastic case.

Scales. Birmingham, Ala.: The Re-Print Corporation.

Available are a personal scale, which has a capacity of 310 pounds; a platform scale, with a removable plastic pan and a capacity of ten pounds; and a simple scale, the balance for which may be adjusted by sliding compensators on the balance arm.

Simple Balance. Rowley, Mass.: Didax Educational Resources.

This balance has a wide pan at each end and a series of ten numbered ridges along each side of the balance arm to hold Unifix Cubes, marbles, and so on.

Simple Scales. Rowley, Mass.: Didax Educational Resources.

The total size of this balance is 18 inches by 12½ inches, with each basket measuring 7¼ inches in diameter. Can be used for measuring liquids and solids up to four pounds. Ten stackable weights are included.

Student's Individual Clocks. Rowley, Mass.: Didax Educational Resources.

These 5½-inch clock faces come in packages of ten and feature movable plastic hour and minute hands.

Tape Measures. Rowley, Mass.: Didax Educational Resources.

Sold in sets of ten, these one-meter tapes have centimeters marked in white on blue.

Telling Time. Big Spring, Tex.: Gamco. Computer diskette for Apple II and MS DOS. Grades K-5. Available from NASCO.

The management system keeps records for as many as 200 students, with names, levels worked, and scores. Includes four lesson styles and different levels of difficulty.

Telling Time Dominoes Set. Columbus, Ohio: Judy/Instructo.

Each of the 64 dominoes features an analog or digital clock face plus time-telling vocabulary. Includes hour and half-hour times as well as quarter-hour, five-minute and minute intervals.

Telling Time Materials. Birmingham, Ala.: The Re-Print Corporation.

Various materials are available, including a digital stopwatch, time flash cards, a clock dial with movable hands, a pupil's clock dial, a class set of 30 clock dials, clock-face stamps, a one-minute sand timer and a mechanical timer, a *Turn-and-Learn* clock, a two-faced clock dial, a perennial calendar chart, a digital learning clock, a *Tell-Time Quismo*, a *Kid Klock*, a clock puzzle, a primary clock and primary miniclocks, *Teaching Time* self-checking classroom clock, *Clock-O-Dial*, and *Time & Money Skills*.

** **Thermometers**. Worth, Ill.: Creative Publications.

Many types of thermometers are available, including: student thermometers in sets of 12; Celsius and Fahrenheit aluminum thermometers in sets of six; overhead-projector-demonstration thermometers marked from minus 40 degrees Fahrenheit to plus 212 degrees Fahrenheit and from minus 40 degrees Celsius to plus 100 degrees Celsius; and an 8-inch-by-24-inch demonstration thermometer with a red-and-white band.

** **Thermometers**. Birmingham, Ala.: The Re-Print Corporation.

Thermometers are available for a variety of purposes. Indoor-outdoor thermometers show indoor and outdoor temperatures in Centigrade and Fahrenheit. Student thermometers are available in packages of 12 with Centigrade and Fahrenheit scales. A jumbo Fahrenheit-Celsius thermometer, 7⅛ inches by 28⅛ inches, helps teach conversions from one scale to another. A demonstration thermometer has a sliding band mounted on heavy cardboard, and a double-scale lab thermometer is 12¼ inches long.

** **Time Big Box**. Blacklick, Ohio: SRA/McGraw Hill. Grades 2-4.

Ready-to-use materials include *Time Tales and Tasks, It's About Time Clocks and Calendars, Flip & Learn Time, Moving Up in Time, Student Clocks, Clock Stamp, Clock Puzzles, Laminated Teaching Clocks,* and *Sequential Picture Cards.* Materials are also available separately.

Time Dominoes. Rowley, Mass.: Didax Educational Resources.

This time-telling set has 24 plastic dominoes to use in practicing telling time at quarter to the hour and quarter after the hour as well as at five-minute intervals such as five past seven.

Time Matching Puzzles. Rowley, MA: Didax Educational Resources.

The set contains 27 puzzles. Each three-piece puzzle shows analog, digital, and written time. The puzzles cover time on the hour; quarter to and after the hour; half hour; five, ten, 20 and 25 minutes before and after the hour.

Time to Time. Rowley, Mass.: Didax Educational Resources.

This set of 48 plastic cards presents 12-hour and 24-hour clock times in analog, digital, and written times. Instructions are included for games and other supplemental activities.

** **Trundle Wheel**. Rowley, Mass.: Didax Educational Resources.

Constructed of heavy plastic with a rubber tire, the wheel clicks to indicate each meter that is measured. The wheel has raised numbers and markings.

Used Numbers Unit. Measuring: From Paces to Feet. Palo Alto, Calif.: Dale Seymour Publications. By Rebecca B. Corwin and Susan Jo Russell. Grades 3-4.

Activities ask students to collect, display, and interpret data using different scales of measurement.

Weather Boards. Buffalo, N.Y.: SI Manufacturing Limited.

Today's Weather and *The Weather Monitor* allow students to measure and record such data as the month's rainfall, atmospheric pressure, and temperature.

CHAPTER 11
STATISTICS AND PROBABILITY

In grades K-4, the mathematics curriculum should include experiences with data analysis and probability so that students can:

➤ collect, organize, and describe data;

➤ construct, read, and interpret displays of data;

➤ formulate and solve problems that involve collecting and analyzing data;

➤ explore concepts of chance.

from *Curriculum and Evaluation Standards for School Mathematics*,
National Council of Teachers of Mathematics, 1989.

APPROACHES

Statistics and probability are appropriately taught in the mathematics class, but they are also closely related to the work students do in science and social studies. Teachers should take advantage of these cross-curricular opportunities.

Students may use these mathematical skills, for example, in preparing a science-fair project. They also may notice any number of things in the world around them, become interested, and begin to collect and analyze data. For example, they may chart the barometric readings and high temperatures for a week and then predict readings for the next day.

In social studies, students might be called upon to compare the value of a country's major crops, present its exports and imports in a graphic form, or graph the average annual rainfall for a group of countries.

A student might note how many left-handed students are in a class and from that make a guess as to the number of left-handed students in the entire school. The accuracy of the guess would, of course, depend on the size of the sample and on whether the original sample class was typical in its makeup.

As students gather and work with data, they learn that it comes in varied forms and that it can be collected, organized, and displayed in a variety of ways. They also increase their ability to read and to make charts and graphs. These mathematical skills can then be effectively used in writing reports and in projects in various curricular areas.

RESOURCES

These resources may help teachers and parents provide a rich mathematical environment for children. The titles under "Books" provide background reading and understanding. The books listed under "Other Resources" are primarily for student use and often contain reproducible pages. This section also lists games, manipulatives, videos, sets of materials, and computer programs. There are brief descriptions of each product. Although a supplier is listed, books may also be available directly from publishers, and books and other materials may be available from several distributors.

Although efforts were made to be thorough, this resource list is not exhaustive. There are other companies that carry many fine products. In addition, new products are constantly coming on the market, and some of the items that are included may go out of print or be discontinued in the future.

This resource list, however, provides a range of available resources for teaching statistics and probability.

Addresses of publishers and suppliers are listed in chapter 15.

Books

** Burns, Marilyn. "Statistical Stuff." Part 5 of **Math for Smarty Pants**. Boston: Little, Brown, 1982. 128p.

Freeman, Marji. **Creative Graphing**. 48p. Available from Institute for Math Mania.
   This book provides more than 80 graph themes for which students supply the data from their own experiences. Provides extensive teacher's notes.

Lee, Martin, and Marcia Miller. **Great Graphing: More Than 60 Activities for Collecting, Displaying, and Using Data, Grades 1-4**. Jefferson City, Mo.: Scholastic Professional Books, 1995. 96p.

** Wilson, Jeni, and Lynda Cutting. **It's Time: Celebrating Maths with Projects**. Portsmouth, N.H.: Heinemann, 1993. 112p.

Other Resources
(manipulatives, games, sets, reproducibles, videos, and computer diskettes)

Binostat. Rowley, Mass.: Didax Educational Resources; Vernon Hills, Ill.: ETA.
   This tool gives a visual demonstration of binomial distribution. Balls bounce randomly on pegs down into a tray and then roll into channels on the tray. Included are 150 balls and a manual on probability.

** **Block Graph Kit**. Vernon Hills, Ill.: ETA.

The kit has ten rods labeled from one to 15 that fit into two plastic bases. Also included are 200 plastic cubes in five colors that fit over posts as stacking markers. Can be used to chart probability, graph statistics, and help students visualize relationships.

Cloudburst of Creative Mathematics Activities. Vernon Hills, Ill.: ETA. *Book 1*, Grades 2-4; *Book 2*, Grades 4-6.

Each book contains 90 experiments. A variety of areas are explored, including probability and statistics, problem solving, operations, geometry, and measurement.

** **A Collection of Math Lessons from Grades 1 Through 3**. Sausalito, Calif.: Math Solutions Publications. By Marilyn Burns. 193p. Distributed by Cuisenaire Company of America.

These lessons explore probability, graphing, numbers, geometry, and measurement.

Data, Chance and Probability Activity Book. Vernon Hills, Ill.: ETA. By C. Thorton and G. Jones. Grades 1-3.

Fifty-three cooperative problem-solving activities involve data analysis, probability comparisons, and math modeling. Also available for Grades 4-6 with 55 activities based on real-world situations.

Dealing with Data and Chance Kit for Use with NCTM Addenda Series. Vernon Hills, Ill.: ETA. Grades K-12.

This kit includes NCTM's *Dealing with Data and Chance Book*. Encourages thought-provoking investigations and includes spinners, cards, and various measuring tools to explore chance, data collection, and analysis. Also available as *Kit with Calculators*, which includes four student Calc-U-Vue Calculators.

Developing Skills with Tables and Graphs. Palo Alto, Calif.: Dale Seymour Publications. By Elaine C. Murphy. *Book A*, 64p. Grades 3-5.

Work sheets develop organizational skills. Contains 48 blackline masters.

D.I.M.E. Probability. Buffalo, N.Y.: SI Manufacturing Limited.

Kit A and *Kit B* contain materials to introduce probability, including experiment cards; recording sheets; teacher's guides; and tubes that contain different combinations of dice, number tabs, and colored beads.

Do-It-Yourself Game Maker Kit. Vernon Hills, Ill.: ETA.

This kit contains materials to make games for exploring probability, including three blank game boards, 18 pawns in six colors, six blank dice with labels, three blank spinners, and 100 transparent counters. Also available are numeral dice, polyhedral dice, decahedral dice, dodecahedral dice, octahedral dice, large dot dice, regular dot dice, blank dice, number cubes, game pawns, blank dice and label sets, spinners, overhead spinners, overhead dice, overhead playing cards, giant foam dice, rubber dice, fraction dice, and place-value cubes.

Graph Paper. Vernon Hills, Ill.: ETA.

Paper is available as 100-sheet metric graph paper; 500-sheet metric graph paper; one-inch graph paper on rolls, which measure 34½ inches in width by 200 feet in length; and one-centimeter graph paper measuring 30 inches in width by 100 feet in length. Also available are graph-paper masters, which contain reproducible graphs for sketching and measurement activities.

 Graph Power. Grover Beach, Calif.: Ventura Educational Systems. Grades K-8. Available from Dale Seymour Publications.

This Macintosh computer diskette comes with a 144-page teacher's guide and activity sheets that demonstrate compiling six computer-generated graphs.

Graph Stamp Set. Vernon Hills, Ill.: ETA.

Available as a set or separately as *Rectangular Coordinates I Stamp*, *Rectangular Coordinates II Stamp*, and *Polar Coordinates Stamp*, each is a rubber three-inch-by-three-inch stamp.

Graphing Fun Reproducible Book. Columbus, Ohio: Judy/Instructo. 20p. Grades 5-8.

This is a good lead-in to students collecting their own data and creating their own graphs. Teaches students to read, plot points, and interpret line graphs.

Graphing Mat. Columbus, Ohio: Judy/Instructo.

This heavy-duty white vinyl mat is 35 inches by 55½ inches. The grid squares measure 5¼ inches by seven inches. It can be used to teach classification, counting, and beginning graphing skills.

Graphing Primer. Palo Alto, Calif.: Dale Seymour Publications. By Laura Duncan Choate. 96p. Grades K-2.

This book helps students learn to tally, record information, and to read and interpret graphs.

Great Explorations in Math and Science (GEMS) in All Probability Teacher's Guide. Berkeley, Calif.: University of California, Lawrence Hall of Science. 99p.

This resource book helps students explore probability and statistics.

Great Graphing. Vernon Hills, Ill.: ETA. 96p. Grades 2-6.

This book contains hands-on activities using pictographs, bar graphs, line graphs, tally charts, scattergrams, and frequency tables.

Grid and Bear It. Vernon Hills, Ill.: ETA. By W. Howell. Grades 1-3.

These activities are carried out on one-inch and ½-inch grids. They enhance skills in listening and following directions.

Grid and Graph It. Vernon Hills, Ill.: ETA. By W. Howell. Grades 4-6.

Gives practice in coordinate geometry using directions and ordered pairs. Includes blackline masters for ½-inch and ¼-inch grids.

Hands-on Statistics, Probability and Graphing. Vernon Hills, Ill.; ETA.

The *Primary* book is for Grades K-2. The *Intermediate* book is for Grades 3-8. Each book contains activity-oriented lessons to teach statistics and probability.

** **In All Probability**. Montpelier, Vt.: Institute for Math Mania. By GEMS Project Staff. Grades 3-6.

Students play games and investigate chance and probability.

** **Math by All Means. Probability: Grades 3-4**. Sausalito, Calif.: Math Solutions
   Publications, 1995. By Marilyn Burns. Also available from Dale Seymour
   Publications.

Students learn to make predictions and test them using number cubes, dice,
spinners, tiles, and counters.

Math-O-Graphs. Pacific Grove, Calif.: Critical Thinking Press & Software. By
   D. Buck and F. Hildebrand. 174p. Grades 4-8.

This book teaches students how to create and use graphic representations to
help solve math problems. It goes across the curriculum into language arts and
science and contains reproducibles.

Oversized Playing Cards. Vernon Hills, Ill.: ETA.

The laminated playing-card deck features extra large symbols and numbers,
with different colored backgrounds for each suit. Designed to promote exploration
of probability concepts. An activity book is included.

Point to Point. Vernon Hills, Ill.: ETA. By G. Munro and A. Munro. Grades 1-6.
Sixteen activities introduce and reinforce graphing skills.

Probability Jobcards: Intermediate. Worth, Ill.: Creative Publications. By Shirley
   Hoogenboom and Judy Goodnow. Grades 3-6.

The 20-card set includes probability experiments for which students collect,
organize, and display data in tables and charts. Includes solutions and a teacher's
guide. Also comes as a *Starter Set* with the *Probability Jobcards* plus 500 rainbow
centimeter cubes, 20 spinners for the overhead projector, 12 pairs of dice, 12
polyhedral dice, and one set of plastic play-money coins.

** **Probability Kit**. Rowley, Mass.: Didax Educational Resources.

This kit allows students to investigate random and selective sampling,
binomial expansion, and binomial distributions. The kit has a binostat with 150
balls, six sample bottles, sampling beads, 24 dice, six large dice, shakers, one set
of playing cards, and a manual on probability.

** **Probability Kit**. Vernon Hills, Ill.: ETA.

Students examine concepts of randomness, chance, and probability through
self-directing experiments. Kit contains activity cards, number cubes, color number
cubes, polyhedral dice, color spinners, number spinners, and school-money coins.

Probability Model Masters. Palo Alto, Calif.: Dale Seymour Publications. By Dale
   Seymour. 128p. All grades.

This publication contains 100 transparency masters for modeling probability
concepts. Also includes playing cards, spinners, dice, and blackline masters.

Quadice. Berkeley, Calif.: University of California, Lawrence Hall of Science, 1993.
   By E. Stage, et al. 56p. Grades 4-8. Also available from Dale Seymour
   Publications.

This game encourages students to make probability predictions and solve
puzzles. Includes teacher instructions and reproducible puzzle sheets.

Statistics and Probability. Vernon Hills, Ill.: ETA. Grades 4-8.

This manipulative kit contains enough materials for a class of 20 to 30
students. Connects math with other content areas and real-world applications.

Included are coins, dice, counters, cubes, spinners, graphing paper, grids, binostat, Versa-Tiles, overhead materials, and resource books.

** **Used Numbers: Real Data in the Classroom.** Palo Alto, Calif.: Dale Seymour Publications. By Susan Jo Russell and Rebecca Corwin. Grades K-6.

This is a project of Technical Education Research Centers, Lesley College, and the Consortium for Mathematics and Its Applications. Each book is a unit of investigation that will take about 15 class sessions. Included are *Counting: Ourselves and Our Families*, Grades K-1, 73p., also available as a *Kit* with LinkerCubes and grid-paper pads; *Sorting: Groups and Graphs*, Grades 2-3, 121p., also available as a *Kit* with LinkerCubes, grid-paper pads, and tubs; *Measuring: From Paces to Feet*, Grades 3-4, 81p.; *Statistics: The Shape of the Data*, Grades 4-6, 82p., also available as a *Kit* with LinkerCubes, meter rules, double-sided measuring tapes, and grid-paper pads; *Statistics: Prediction and Sampling*, Grades 5-6, 104p., also available as a *Kit* with ten double-sided measuring tapes, counting chips, and grid-paper pads; *Statistics: Middles, Means, and In-Betweens*, Grades 5-6, 88p. Also sold as a series.

What Are My Chances? Worth, Ill.: Creative Publications. By Albert P. Shulte and Stuart A. Choate. *Book A*, 112p. Grades 4-6.

This book contains 70 hands-on activities and experiments that require students to think about a situation, predict possible results, and compare results. Also includes reproducibles.

What Are My Chances? Probability Kit A. Worth, Ill.: Creative Publications. Grades 4-9.

This kit includes *What Are My Chances?* book and 600 transparent chips, 12 pairs of ½-inch dice, ten spinners for the overhead projects, eight sets of polyhedral dice, eight packs of playing cards, and one set of play-money coins.

World Series Golf. Rowley, Mass.: Didax Educational Resources.

Multiplication, probability, negative numbers, and data-handling skills are involved in this game for two to 12 players.

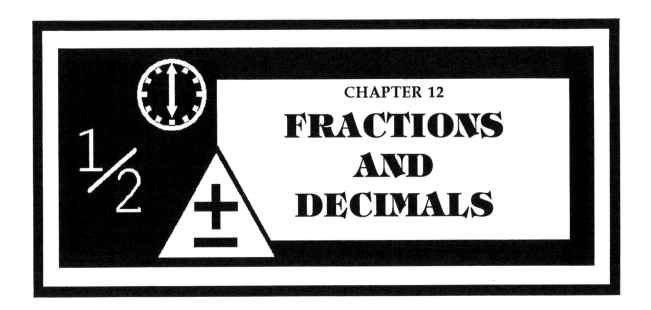

CHAPTER 12

FRACTIONS AND DECIMALS

In grades K-4, the mathematics curriculum should include fractions and decimals so that students can:

➤ develop concepts of fractions, mixed numbers, and decimals;

➤ develop number sense for fractions and decimals;

➤ use models to relate fractions to decimals and to find equivalent fractions;

➤ use models to explore operations on fractions and decimals;

➤ apply fractions and decimals to problem situations.

from *Curriculum and Evaluation Standards for School Mathematics*,
National Council of Teachers of Mathematics, 1989.

APPROACHES

Many practical, everyday situations will come up in the elementary-school classroom to help children learn about and apply their knowledge of fractions. During a snack time, they might divide a whole apple into equal parts for five children at a table. During an art project, they may need to fold a piece of paper into fourths or thirds. Understanding the concepts involved in a unit and its equal subdivisions is fundamental to understanding fractions and decimals.

Students need many opportunities not only to divide a whole into parts but also to put parts together to make up a whole. As they work with manipulatives, students see that one-third is larger than one-eighth and gradually come to understand the relative size of fractions.

When students work with sums of money, metric measures, and calculators, they soon encounter decimals in their activities. Gradually students learn to establish connections between decimals and fractions, recognizing that .5 is one-half and that .6 is more than one-half.

RESOURCES

These resources may help teachers and parents provide a rich mathematical environment for children. The titles under "Books" provide background reading and understanding. The books listed under "Other Resources" are primarily for student use and often contain reproducible pages. This section also lists games, manipulatives, videos, sets of materials, and computer programs. There are brief descriptions of each product. Although a supplier is listed, books may also be available directly from publishers, and books and other materials may be available from several distributors.

Although efforts were made to be thorough, this resource list is not exhaustive. There are other companies that carry many fine products. In addition, new products are constantly coming on the market, and some of the items that are included may go out of print or be discontinued in the future.

This resource list, however, provides a range of available resources for teaching fractions and decimals.

Addresses of publishers and suppliers are listed in chapter 15.

Books

Balka, Don. **Exploring Fractions and Decimals with Manipulatives**. Rowley, Mass.: Didax Educational Resources, 1994. 54p.

Barnett, C., D. Goldenstein, and B. Jackson, eds. **Fractions, Decimals, Ratios, and Percents**. Portsmouth, N.H.: Heinemann, 1994. 122p. Grade 4 and up.
This book uses a case-discussion approach and was written by upper-elementary and middle-school teachers. It is available as a set, casebook only, or with a facilitator's discussion guide with suggestions for initiating faculty discussion groups.

** Kelleher, Heather J. **Mathworks Book B**. Boston: Houghton Mifflin, 1992. 400p.
This book includes a section on money and decimals.

Van de Walle, John A. **Elementary School Mathematics: Teaching Developmentally**. 2d ed. White Plains, N.Y.: Longman, 1994. 544p.
Chapters 13 and 14 address fractions and decimals.

** Wilson, Jeni, and Lynda Cutting. **It's Time: Celebrating Maths with Projects**. Portsmouth, N.H.: Heinemann, 1993. 112p.

Other Resources

(manipulatives, games, sets, reproducibles, videos, and computer diskettes)

Action Fraction Games. Columbus, Ohio: Judy/Instructo. Grade 1 and up.
This set includes eight game boards with fractional cubes and instructions for five games.

BandCulator. Richardson, Tex.: Kaidy Educational Resources. Grades 3-8.
This device allows students to stretch rubber bands around pegs to create pie-shaped wedges representing fractions.

BarCulator. Richardson, Tex.: Kaidy Educational Resources. Grades 3-8.

The teaching tool demonstrates fraction relationships using a BarCulator ruler and bars representing fractions. Also available for overhead projectors and in a giant demonstration format for teacher use.

Basic Math Games. Palo Alto, Calif.: Dale Seymour Publications. By George Bright and John Harvey.

The set contains two books, dice, and chips. The games are designed to teach basic math facts, including ordering fractions and operations on fractions.

** **Coin and Paper Bill Sets**. Palo Alto, Calif.: Dale Seymour Publications.

Colossal Money Combo Pack includes large reproductions of U.S. money. *Money for the Overhead Projector* is available separately in coins and bills. *Money and Mathematics*, Prentice Hall, Grade 4 and up, is an illustrated dictionary with 800 entries. *Money Jobcards*, by Ann Roper, Grades 1-3, is a set of activity cards to help students learn about money, but the play money must be purchased separately.

** **Constructing Ideas About Fractions: Grades 3-6**. Worth, Ill.: Creative Publications. By Julie Pier Brodie. 112p.

The activities included require students to use manipulatives to learn about fractions. The set contains reproducibles and can also be purchased as a *Classroom Kit* and as a *Starter Kit*, which include the necessary manipulatives.

Decimal Fraction Dominoes. Rowley, Mass.: Didax Educational Resources.

This game contains 24 plastic dominoes and provides practice in fraction and decimal recognition.

Developing Mathematical Thinking: Fractions. Portland, Oreg.: MESD Press, 1991. By Jay Greenwood. 246p. Also available from Dale Seymour Publications.

This 81-lesson series on fractions includes a teacher's guide and reproducible work sheets.

Equivalence Dominoes. Rowley, Mass.: Didax Educational Resources.

This dominoes game provides practice in recognizing fractional shapes and expressing them as fractions and decimal equivalents. Available separately are *Equivalence Cards*, a set of 48 plastic playing cards that require students to match numbers and figures expressed as fractions, decimals, and percentages.

Equivalent Fraction Shapes. Rowley, Mass.: Didax Educational Resources.

Twenty-four plastic triangles are matched on each side to equivalent fractions to reinforce understanding. Instructions are included.

Equivalent Fractions Matching Cards. Rowley, Mass.: Didax Educational Resources.

The set includes 112 two-color cards. The cards illustrate segments of a circle, divisions of a square, and subdivisions of a whole and can be used for many activities and games.

✱✱ **Exploring Fractions and Decimals Kit**. Rowley, Mass.: Didax Educational Resources.

The kit provides a teacher's guide to assist students with concrete and symbolic representations of fractions. Included are fraction squares and circles, overhead fraction squares and circles, visual fraction discs, equivalent fractions matching cards, decimal fraction dominoes, equivalence cards, equivalent fraction shapes, percentage fraction shapes, fractions-lowest terms, fractions stamps, dice, and dominoes.

Fit-a-Fraction Circles. Birmingham, Ala.: The Re-Print Corporation. Grades K-4.

This set of foam-rubber circles shows wholes, halves, thirds, fourths, fifths, sixths, eighths, and tenths. Also includes a rubber frame and underlay cards.

FraConcepts. Richardson, Tex.: Kaidy Educational Resources.

This series is dedicated to understanding and manipulating fractions. Included are *FracNaming*, Grades 2-6, with 28 task cards and activities; *FracChart*, Grades 3-9, with task cards; *Overhead Transparencies*; *FracMulti*, Grades 3-9, three-inch-by-five-inch cards with transparent overlays to produce problems for demonstrating multiplication of fractions; *FracDivide*, Grades 3-8, with overhead transparencies and interchangeable three-inch-by-five-inch cards and transparent overlays to demonstrate division of fractions; and *Math Wrap-ups*, which use string to match an item on the left side with its equivalent on the right side so that when correctly done, it can be turned over to reveal the string covering up a set of lines on the plastic card.

Fraction Activity Cards. Birmingham, Ala.: The Re-Print Corporation.

These 5¼-inch-by-4½-inch cards include pictorial depictions of common fractions on one side and the written form of the fraction on the other. These can be used with *Circular Fraction Set*, *Overhead Circular Fraction Set*, *Square Fraction Set*, and *Overhead Fraction Squares*.

Fraction Bars Classroom Management Center. Palo Alto, Calif.: Dale Seymour Publications. Grades 3-6.

With materials for up to 28 students, this complete set includes fraction bars; playing cards; activity mats, including Bingo, Small Step Race, Capture, Number Lines, Dots, and Tower of Bars; spinners; dice; game markers; and overhead fraction bars. *Fraction Bars Starter Set* contains fraction bars, a teacher's guide, markers, and color transparencies. Parts are also available separately.

Fraction Cakes Game. Columbus, Ohio: Judy/Instructo.

This game helps students identify and match fractional parts from one-half to one-tenth. Spinner and instructions for several games are included.

Fraction Circle Activities. Palo Alto, Calif.: Dale Seymour Publications. By Barbara Berman and Fredda Friederwitzer. 64p. Grades 4-8.

This collection of 44 blackline masters requires the use of fraction circles. *Fraction Circles and Squares* are brightly colored plastic models to help students visualize and understand fractional parts. *Fraction Circle Rings* fit around fraction circles and can be purchased separately to show decimals, degrees, or time.

Fraction Circles. Columbus, Ohio: Judy/Instructo.

This 24-piece set contains six vinyl circles measuring 3½ inches in diameter to represent different fractional parts. *Overhead Fraction Circles* are also available.

Fraction Concepts, Inc. Minneapolis, Minn.: MECC/Softkey International. Computer diskette for Apple II, II Plus, IIe, IIc, IIgs. Also available from NASCO.

Students playing this game work in a fraction factory where workers visualize the functions of numerators and denominators, recognize equivalent fractions, and add fractions to make a whole. Includes a teacher's guide.

Fraction Dice. Worth, Ill.: Creative Publications. Grades 3-8.

A set of four dice include one-fourth, one-third, one-half, one-sixth, one-eighth, and $\frac{1}{12}$ on one two-pair set and one-half, two-thirds, three-fourths, five-sixths, seven-eighths, and $\frac{11}{12}$ printed in black on white on the other set.

Fraction Flip Books and Activity Cards. Rowley, Mass.: Didax Educational Resources. Grades 3-6.

Activity cards and three eight-inch-by-two-inch laminated flip books provide fraction exercises for independent student use.

Fraction Games. Birmingham, Ala.: The Re-Print Corporation.

The set includes wholes, halves, thirds, fourths, sixths, and eighths. Comes with instructions for games at two levels of fraction understanding.

Fraction Match-up. Birmingham, Ala.: The Re-Print Corporation. Grades 3-6.

This card game gives students practice in matching equivalent fractions.

 ** **Fraction Munchers.** Minneapolis, Minn.: MECC/Softkey International. Computer diskette for Apple II, II Plus, IIe, IIc, IIgs. Grade 3 and up. Also available from NASCO.

Students help the Munchers against the Troggles while practicing various types of fractional numbers. Includes a teacher's guide.

** **Fraction Pieces.** Worth, Ill.: Creative Publications. Grades 3-8.

Fraction Circles Plus contains 51 pieces and can be purchased as one set, nine sets, with overhead circles, and with picture grids. *Activities for Fraction Circles Plus*, 176p., by Ann Roper and Linda Holden Charles, contains 140 sequenced fraction activities. *Jobcards for Fraction Circles Plus*, by Ann Roper and Linda Holden Charles, come in four sets with 22 activities each. The sets include *Naming Fractions*, *Comparing Fractions*, *Adding and Subtracting Fractions*, and *Multiplying and Dividing Fractions*. *Thinking Questions for Fraction Circles Plus*, Grades 3-6, is a 112-page resource book. *Fraction Squares Plus* is a set of 51 pieces and can be purchased as one set, nine sets, with overhead squares, and with picture grids. *Fraction Factory Pieces* is sold as a 51-piece set and is available as one set, nine sets, with overheads, and with picture grids. *Fraction Factory Games & Puzzles*, Grades 3-8, contains 15 games. *Fraction Factory Jobcards*, by Ann Roper and Linda Holden Charles, come in four sets to give students practice with naming fractions, comparing fractions, adding and subtracting fractions, and multiplying and dividing fractions; *Fraction Builder* is sold as a 51-piece set, as a bucket of nine sets, with overheads, and with picture grids. Also available is *Cooperative Problem Solving with Fraction Pieces*, Grades 4-6, which can be bought as a *Classroom Set* with materials for eight groups of four students.

Fraction Pieces. Buffalo, N.Y.: SI Manufacturing Limited.

These are sets of rectangular pieces representing halves, thirds, quarters, fifths, sixths, eighths, tenths, and 12ths. A teacher's guide is included.

Fraction Squares. Columbus, Ohio: Judy/Instructo.

Set contains 24 pieces. All fractional parts equal one whole square. Available in opaque or as overhead transparencies.

Fraction Squares and **Fraction Circles**. Rowley, Mass.: Didax Educational Resources.

The square set contains eight complete four-inch plastic squares in fractions of one-half, one-sixth, one-third, one-fourth, and one whole. The circles set contains eight plastic circles in fractions of one-half, one-third, one-fourth, one-fifth, one-sixth, one-eighth, one-tenth, and one whole.

Fraction Stax. Birmingham, Ala.: The Re-Print Corporation.

A set includes 51 pieces, a nine-peg base, and a teacher's guide. The pieces model one whole, halves, thirds, fourths, fifths, sixths, eighths, tenths, and 12ths. Also available is a *Fraction Stax Naming and Comparing Kit* and *Fraction Stax Addition and Subtraction Kit*.

Fraction Strips. Palo Alto, Calif.: Dale Seymour Publications. Grades K-8.

The color-coded pieces are available in halves, thirds, fourths, sixths, eighths, and 12ths. Also available as *Overhead Fraction Strips*.

Fraction Strips. Columbus, Ohio: Judy/Instructo.

Nine strips in different colors, show wholes, halves, thirds, fourths, fifths, sixths, eighths, tenths, and 12ths. Available in opaque or for the overhead projector.

Fraction Tiles: A Manipulative Fraction Program. Hayward, Calif.: Activity Resources Company, 1972. By Lee Jenkins and Peggy McLean. Grades 2-9. Also available from Dale Seymour Publications.

The complete set includes *transparent plastic tiles* in seven colors, a manipulative book, student book, and teacher's book. The various components are also available separately.

Fraction Tray. Birmingham, Ala.: The Re-Print Corporation. Grades K-4.

Students fill the wooden tray with parts of a circle, including wholes, halves, thirds, and fourths.

Fractions. Palo Alto, Calif.: Dale Seymour Publications.

Players roll fraction dice and place fraction pieces together to complete a circle. Includes 32 playing pieces.

Fractions Are As Easy As Pie. Birmingham, Ala.: The Re-Print Corporation. Grades 2-6.

This game teaches fractions as students race to build a whole pie.

Fractions Kit. Rowley, Mass.: Didax Educational Resources.

This kit contains materials to help students understand fractions. Included are self-correcting cards, fraction games, and matching activities using discs, cards, flip books, dominoes, and rubber stamps. A teacher's guide is provided.

Fractions—Lowest Terms. Rowley, Mass.: Didax Educational Resources.

This dominoes game for two to four players contains 24 plastic tiles that students use to match fractions to their lowest-term equivalents.

Fractions Set 1. Rowley, Mass.: Didax Educational Resources.

Twenty pairs of laminated, self-correcting cards illustrate wholes, halves, eighths, and thirds.

Fractions Set 2. Rowley, Mass.: Didax Educational Resources.

This set includes an inset board, manipulative fraction pieces, problem cards, and answer cards.

Fractions with Pattern Blocks. Worth, Ill.: Creative Publications. By Matthew E. Zullie. 126p. Grades 3-6.

This book contains a wide range of pattern-block activities on perforated, reproducible work sheets. Pattern blocks are required.

Geometric Fraction Shapes. Palo Alto, Calif.: Dale Seymour Publications.

This set of 64 plastic pieces in four colors helps students explore halves, thirds, and quarters.

Math Games & Activities. Palo Alto, Calif.: Dale Seymour Publications. By Paul Shoecraft. *Vol. 1*, 332p.; *Vol. 2*, 448p.

Each volume features more than 300 reproducible games, activity work sheets, and aids. Many topics are included, such as fractions, decimals, and percents.

Money. Birmingham, Ala.: The Re-Print Corporation.

Available are *Mixed Coins, Calculator Cash Register, Fun with Money Activity Book, Jumbo Assortment of Toy Coins, Money Matters Workbook, Money Flash Cards, Dollars & Cents Kit for the Flannelboard, Classroom Cash, Money Math Cards, Jumbo Assortment of Toy Bills, Megabucks, Cashbox, Colossal Coins, Colossal Currency, Combo Pack, Coin Matching Cards,* and *Making Change Cards*.

** Money Classroom Kit. Worth, Ill.: Creative Publications. Grades PreK-3.

This set includes books, two buckets of play money, and one set each of overhead coins and bills. Available separately are *Play Money Coins, Bucket of Coins, Coins for the Overhead Projector, Play Money Bills Mini Set, Play Money Bills Complete Set, Overhead Bills Deluxe Set, Play Money Coins and Bills Combination Pack, Bucket of Play Money,* and *Money Rubber Stamps. Money Jobcards,* by Ann Roper, includes 22 activity cards for *Counting Coins* or for *Problem Solving with Coins.* These are also packaged with coins and as a set, *Money Jobcards Starter Set*.

Money Matters. Birmingham, Ala.: The Re-Print Corporation. Grades 3-6.

The set includes 50 activities on five-inch-by-eight-inch cards that give practice with consumer skills. Coins, bills, and a poster are included.

Multilink Fraction Activities. Glen Burnie, Md.: NES Arnold. By B. Stone, L. Frobisher, and P. Patilla. *Book 1* and *Book 2*, each 32p. Grades 4-5. Available from Dale Seymour Publications.

The books contain blackline masters for teaching fractions using *Multilink Cubes* and *Prisms*, which can be purchased separately.

Number Fraction Dominoes. Rowley, Mass.: Didax Educational Resources.

These dominoes have two levels of difficulty and provide practice with fractions.

** **Pattern Blocks**. Worth, Ill.: Creative Publications. Grades K-9.

Packed in a bucket, the 250 pattern blocks are available in wood or plastic and can be used with the book *Fractions with Pattern Blocks* to explore fractions. Also available as a set, which includes the book.

Percentage Fraction Shapes. Rowley, Mass.: Didax Educational Resources.

Students match percentages and fractions using 24 plastic triangles. Instructions for play are included.

PieCulator. Richardson, Tex.: Kaidy Educational Resources. Grades 3-8.

This is a hands-on teaching tool for demonstrating fraction relationships using a plastic PieCulator and set of colorful pie pieces representing different fractions. *Teacher's PieCulator* is available in a large size and is made of felt. Also available is *FraCard*, a deck of 59 playing cards, with instructions for five games using fractions.

Pizza Party. Birmingham, Ala.: The Re-Print Corporation. Grade 2 and up.

The game kit contains 12 pizzas that are divided into halves, fourths, thirds, sixths, eighths, ninths, 12ths, and 16ths. Also includes spinners and a booklet for eight games.

Presto Change-O! Birmingham, Ala.: The Re-Print Corporation. Grades 3-6.

The set includes a game board, dice, game pawns, markers, realistic bills, and coins. For two to four players. Teaches students to make change quickly.

Primary Cooperative Problem Solving with Coins. Worth, Ill.: Creative Publications. By Ann Roper.

The 72 reproducible hands-on activities use coins in real-life problem solving. Coins are sold separately. *Resolver Problemas en Cooperacion*, the Spanish version, is also available.

** **Rainbow Fraction Tiles**. Birmingham, Ala.: The Re-Print Corporation. Grades 2-6.

The 51 proportional plastic pieces represent a whole, halves, thirds, fourths, fifths, sixth, eighths, tenths, and 12ths that fit in a 9-inch-by-12-inch tray. Comes with teacher's guide.

School Money Starter Kit. Rowley, Mass.: Didax Educational Resources.

Set includes a change drawer and play coins and bills. School bills and coins can also be bought separately in packages of 100 each or in mixed sets.

Square Parts. Rowley, Mass.: Didax Educational Resources.

The eight-inch-by-eight-inch matrix and fraction pieces allow students to fit various fraction pieces together to form wholes.

Visual Fraction Discs. Rowley, Mass.: Didax Educational Resources.

Each segment of these colored three-inch plastic discs has a fraction printed as a figure on one side and the word on the reverse. Included are wholes, halves, quarters, and thirds.

CHAPTER 13

PATTERNS AND RELATIONSHIPS

In grades K-4, the mathematics curriculum should include the study of patterns and relationships so that students can:

➤ recognize, describe, extend, and create a wide variety of patterns;

➤ represent and describe mathematical relationships;

➤ explore the use of variables and open sentences to express relationships.

from *Curriculum and Evaluation Standards for School Mathematics*,
National Council of Teachers of Mathematics, 1989.

APPROACHES

The classroom provides many opportunities for students to explore patterns. They will come to recognize regularities in shapes, designs, and sets of numbers. Young students may string beads in a pattern involving color and sometimes size. Teachers may also involve them in an art project for which they repeat a pattern, repeat a shape but change the color, or repeat a shape but change its orientation.

Students may be asked to notice patterns in the fabric of people's clothing, in quilts and wall hangings, or in wallpaper borders. They also may be given a set of numbers such as 6, 9, 12, 15 and be asked what number would come next in this pattern.

As students grow in their ability to work with patterns, they learn to represent them geometrically and numerically. This helps students make connections between arithmetic and geometry.

Relating patterns to numbers helps students see connections among mathematical topics and promotes a kind of mathematical thinking that will be a foundation for more abstract ideas that are studied in later grades.

RESOURCES

These resources may help teachers and parents provide a rich mathematical environment for children. The titles under "Books" provide background reading and understanding. The books listed under "Other Resources" are primarily for student use and often contain reproducible pages. This section also lists games, manipulatives, videos, sets of materials, and computer programs. There are brief descriptions of each product. Although a supplier is listed, books may also be available directly from publishers, and books and other materials may be available from several distributors.

Although efforts were made to be thorough, this resource list is not exhaustive. There are other companies that carry many fine products. In addition, new products are constantly coming on the market, and some of the items that are included may go out of print or be discontinued in the future.

This resource list, however, provides a range of available resources for teaching patterns and relationships.

Addresses of publishers and suppliers are listed in chapter 15.

Books

✱✱ Abrohms, Alison. **1001 Instant Manipulatives for Math, Grades Pre K-2**. Jefferson City, Mo.: Scholastic Professional Books, 1995. 128p.

✱✱ Burk, Donna, Allyn Snider, and Paula Symonds. **Math Excursions Series, K, 1, 2**. Portsmouth, N.H.: Heinemann, 1992. *Grade K*, 266p.; *Grade 1*, 259p; *Grade 2*, 218p.

Walter, Marion. **Look at Annette**. New York: M. Evans & Company, 1977. 32p. Grades 1-3. Also available from Dale Seymour Publications.
This hardcover book comes with a metal mirror and helps young children view and learn about patterns and symmetry.

Wilson, Jeni, and Lynda Cutting. **It's Time: Celebrating Maths with Projects**. Portsmouth, N.H.: Heinemann, 1993. 112p.

Other Resources

(manipulatives, games, sets, reproducibles, videos, and computer diskettes)

✱✱ About Teaching Mathematics. Sausalito, Calif.: Math Solutions Publications, 1992. By Marilyn Burns. 275p. Grades K-8. Distributed by Cuisenaire Company of America.
This book contains more than 240 classroom-tested activities and includes blackline masters. Among the topics covered are patterns, measurement, probability and statistics, geometry, and logic.

✱✱ Attribute Blocks. Buffalo, N.Y.: SI Manufacturing Limited.
Available are standard and related sets in different shapes, thicknesses, sizes, and colors, including overhead blocks and teacher's guides.

Calculators, Patterns and Magic. Montpelier, Vt.: Institute for Math Mania.

Students use a calculator to discover number patterns and check predictions about mathematical patterns.

Color Cubes. Buffalo, N.Y.: SI Manufacturing Limited.

Sets of two-centimeter solid plastic cubes in five colors are included. Instruction cards and a teacher's guide are also available.

Color Tiles. Buffalo, N.Y.: SI Manufacturing Limited.

Student sets and class sets of thick, plastic 2½-centimeter tiles come in four colors. A teacher's guide is available.

Constructing Ideas About Patterns: Grades 1-3. Worth, Ill.: Creative Publications. By Sandra Ward. 112p.

This book includes several activities to give students an understanding of patterns, although many activities require manipulatives. Includes reproducibles.

** **Constructing Ideas About Patterns: Grades 1-3 Classroom Kit**. Worth, Ill.: Creative Publications.

This kit includes the book and LinkerCubes, thin pattern blocks, overhead LinkerCubes, and pattern blocks. Enough materials for 32 students working in pairs. Also available as a *Starter Set* with enough materials for eight students working in pairs.

Giant Pattern Block Floor Tiles. Rowley, Mass.: Didax Educational Resources.

This set includes 12 yellow hexagons, 12 orange squares, 24 green triangles, 24 red trapezoids, 24 blue parallelograms, and 24 brown rhombuses. The squares are four inches by four inches. Tiles are made of polyester carpet with nonslip rubber backing. A teacher's guide is included.

Giant Tangram Floor Tiles. Rowley, Mass.: Didax Educational Resources.

Tiles are made of polyester carpet with nonslip rubber backing. A teacher's guide is included. Completed square tangram shape measures 13 inches by 13 inches.

** **Hands-on Pattern Blocks**. Worth, Ill.: Creative Publications. Grades K-3.

A variety of activity suggestions using pattern blocks are included along with 120 reproducible pages. Also available as a *Hands-on Pattern Blocks Starter Set* with enough blocks for ten students. Pattern blocks available in wood or plastic. Available also in plastic or wood as a *Classroom Kit* with enough materials for a whole class.

Interlocking Cubes. Buffalo, N.Y.: SI Manufacturing Limited.

These cubes are available in one-centimeter/one-gram or two-centimeter sizes. They come in assorted colors and interlock positively on all six sides. Available in packages ranging from 100 to 1,000 pieces.

Kaleidoscope Math. Worth, Ill.: Creative Publications. By Joe Kennedy and Diane Thomas. 120p. Grades 4-10.

This book contains activities that explain how to create a variety of simple kaleidoscopes. Comes with three four-inch-by-six-inch plastic mirrors. Students can form geometric figures and tessellating patterns. Pages are reproducible.

✱✱ = Highly recommended.   **= Computer resources.**   **= Videos.**

Magnetic Manipulatives. Buffalo, N.Y.: SI Manufacturing Limited.

Student boards are available as well as fraction circles, pattern blocks, related attribute blocks, pentominoes, tangrams, power of ten, and color squares.

Matrix Design Stamps. Palo Alto, Calif.; Dale Seymour Publications.

Students may use these washable stamps to explore geometric shapes. Available in different sets with instruction booklets. Ink pads required.

Mental Math in the Middle Grades. Palo Alto, Calif.: Dale Seymour Publications. By J. Hope, B. Reys, and R. Reys. 128p. Grades 4-6.

This book contains 36 lessons to help students do mental arithmetic. Includes practice sets, teaching notes, and transparency masters.

Mental Math in the Primary Grades. Palo Alto, Calif.: Dale Seymour Publications. By J. Hope, L. Leutzinger, B. Reys, and R. Reys. 128p. Grades 1-3.

This book develops understanding of using patterns in the base ten system. Includes 36 lessons with teaching notes, transparencies, and blackline masters.

Moving on with Pattern Blocks. Worth, Ill.: Creative Publications. By Ann Roper. Grades 4-6.

This book contains 112 reproducible activity pages. Also available as a *Starter Set* with materials for eight students and as a *Classroom Kit* with materials for 32 students.

Multivariant Sequencing Beads, Multivariant Sequencing Bead Patterns. Blacklick, Ohio: SRA/McGraw Hill.

** **Pattern Blocks**. Worth, Ill.: Creative Publications. Grades K-9.

Pattern blocks are available in plastic and wood and for the overhead projector. Also available are sets of thin pattern blocks in sets of 100 and buckets of 250. Sets of *20 Thinking Questions for Pattern Blocks* are available for Grades K-3 and for Grades 3-6. This material is also available as a classroom kit and as a starter set with manipulatives. *Pattern Blocks Rubber Stamps* and *Pattern Blocks Stickers* are also available. *Pattern Blocks Tracer* is a plastic template. The *Pattern Block Sampler* includes three buckets of pattern blocks and the 16-page booklet, *Take Off with Pattern Blocks*. *Jobcards with Pattern Blocks*, by Ann Roper, are available in different sets, including *Kindergarten Match & Color*, *Primary Puzzles*, *Primary Patterns*, and *Intermediate Puzzles*. These can also be purchased with manipulatives as a *starter set*. Ann Roper has also written *Cooperative Problem Solving with Pattern Blocks (Grades 1-3)* and an *Intermediate Cooperative Problem Solving with Pattern Blocks (Grades 4-6)*. Each of these is also available in a Spanish version.

 Patterns and Sequence. San Diego, Calif.: Hartley Courseware. Computer diskette for Apple II, II Plus, IIe, IIc. PreK-K. Available from NASCO.

These four math games help young children match abstract shapes and designs as well as single objects with objects in sequence. Includes stickers, stencils, cards, and guide.

Pegboard Math. Vernon Hills, Ill.: ETA. 120p. Grades K-3.

This book contains reproducibles that involve following directions, patterning, counting, and making shapes. Peg boards, wooden pegs, and peg board activity cards are available separately.

Posters. Worth, Ill.: Creative Publications.

These 12-inch-by-12-inch posters illustrate mathematical patterns and concepts. Available are *Math in Nature Posters*, *Math in the Sky Posters*, *Stained Glass Tessellation Posters*, and *Earthshapes Posters*. Each comes with an information sheet, brochure, or booklet.

✶✶ Primary and **Intermediate Jobcards Puzzles with Tangrams**. Worth, Ill.: Creative Publications. By Ann Roper. Grades PreK-6.

Each set features puzzles using tangram pieces. The tangrams are sold separately. *Primary Jobcards Tangram Starter Set* includes the puzzles and eight sets of tangrams. *The Intermediate Jobcards Tangram Starter Set* includes the puzzles and eight sets of tangrams. Also available for Grades 4-6 by Ann Roper are *Cooperative Problem Solving with Tangrams* in Spanish and English and *Cooperative Problem Solving with Tangrams Class Kits*, which includes 16 sets of tangrams. *Tangram Patterns*, 159p., Grades K-12, contains 200 tangram puzzles. *Tangramath*, Grades 1-10, 114p., contains reproducible activity sheets with many activities.

Quilt Design Masters. Palo Alto, Calif.: Dale Seymour Publications. By Luanne Seymour Cohen. 152p. Grades 3-10.

With listings of more than 400 historical quilt patterns, this resource suggests ways to integrate these into the curriculum. Contains blackline masters.

Reasoning, Patterns & Relationships Kit. Vernon Hills, Ill.: ETA. Grades K-4.

The kit contains enough materials for a class of 20 to 30 students. Enables students to make and describe patterns with geometric shapes and with numbers. Materials include pattern blocks, attribute blocks, links, color tiles, Popcubes, hundred boards, grouping circles, activity cards, Versa-Tiles, and resource books.

Star Mosaics. Palo Alto, Calif.: Dale Seymour Publications. By Jonathan Quintin. This 11-inch-by-11-inch book contains 30 reproducible designs.

Super Tangrams. Worth, Ill.: Creative Publications. Grades 4-12.

These sets contain 14 shapes made by combining four isosceles right triangles. A set contains 14 plastic pieces. *Super Tangram Activities*, by Henri Picciotto, Grades 4-8, helps students look at shapes in new ways. *Book 1* contains 48 pages and introduces the names of the shapes.

✶✶ TableTop Tessellations Design Sheets. Worth, Ill.: Creative Publications. Grades K-8.

Set A and *Set B* each contains ten 17-inch-by-22-inch sheets of six patterns. Also available is a *TableTop Tessellations Design Kit*, which includes the same design sheets plus a bucket of 432 rainbow pattern blocks. The *TableTop Tessellations with Pattern Blocks Kit* contains the 17-inch-by-22-inch design sheets and two buckets of 250-count thin pattern blocks. The *Tessellations Exploration Pack*, Grades 2-12, contains a template and 180 plastic pieces in two colors and in nonregular tessellating shapes with sizes from one inch to four inches. *Tessellation Tracer* is a plastic template that contains two sizes of regular three-, four-, five-, six-, eight-, ten- and 12-sided polygons plus some nontessellating polygons.

✶✶ Tangrams. Palo Alto, Calif.: Dale Seymour Publications.

Tangrams are available in two-set or 20-set packages. *Transparent Tangrams* are available for use with the overhead projector. *ESS Tangram Cards* (The Elementary Science Study), Grades K-8, contain three sets of tangram cards with all 121 patterns from the original Elementary Science Study project. They are available separately or as a package of three sets. *Tangrams: 330 Puzzles*, by Ronald Read, Grades 1-8, contain puzzles and solutions involving geometric patterns, letters, numbers, animals, and so on. *Tangoes* are self-contained sets of seven tangram pieces with 54 puzzle cards. Also available are two extra card sets. *Tangramath*, by Dale Seymour, Grades 1-10, contains reproducible activities for exploring with tangrams.

Tessellation Shapes. Palo Alto, Calif.: Dale Seymour Publications. Grade 3 and up.
These many-colored plastic shapes provide for hands-on tessellating. Available in different packages and as templates.

 TesselMania! Minneapolis, Minn.: MECC/Softkey International. Grades 2-12. Also available from Dale Seymour Publications.
This software program for the Macintosh LC or later versions introduces students to tessellations.

Wooden Pattern Blocks. Boulder, Colo.: PlayFair Toys.
This set contains 250 pattern blocks in assorted sizes. *Communicating Math with Pattern Blocks Books, Beginner* and *Intermediate* are also available.

CHAPTER 14
RESOURCES FOR USE ACROSS THE NCTM STANDARDS

Addresses of publishers and suppliers are listed in chapter 15.

Books

** Anno, Mitsumasa. **Anno's Math Games**. New York: Philomel, 1987. 104p. Grades PreK-3. Also available from Dale Seymour Publications.
This book focuses on comparing, classifying, combining, adding, subtracting, sequencing, measuring, and graphing.

** ———. **Anno's Math Games III**. New York: Philomel, 1991. 103p. Grades K-3. Also available from Dale Seymour Publications.
This book presents abstracting to look at things from different perspectives.

Balka, Don S. **Show Me: Assessment with Unifix Cubes**. Rowley, Mass.: Didax Educational Resources, 1995. 64p.

** Burns, Marilyn. **About Teaching Mathematics**. Sausalito, Calif.: Math Solutions Publications, 1992. 304p. Distributed by Cuisenaire Company of America.
This book provides math-standard explorations, which serve as models for classroom problem-solving experiences.

Cooney, Thomas, and Christian R. Hirsch, eds. **Teaching and Learning Mathematics in the 1990s**. Reston, Va.: National Council of Teachers of Mathematics, 1990. 256p. Grades K-8. Also available from Dale Seymour Publications.
Essays on trends and developments in teaching mathematics are featured.

Cuevas, Gilbert, and Mark Driscoll, eds. **Reaching All Students with Mathematics**. Reston, Va.: National Council of Teachers of Mathematics, 1993. 256p. Grades K-12. Also available from Dale Seymour Publications.
Seventeen essays outline current programs designed to reach all students through new approaches to mathematics.

Dahlke, Richard, and Roger Verhey. **What Expert Teachers Say About Teaching Mathematics**. Palo Alto, Calif.: Dale Seymour Publications, 1986. 176p. Grades K-8.

This book was drawn from a questionnaire answered by 50 master teachers.

Davidson, Neil, ed. **Cooperative Learning in Mathematics**. Reading, Mass.: Addison Wesley Longman, 1990. 416p. Also available from Dale Seymour Publications.

This collection of essays concerns practical strategies for using small groups in mathematics teaching and learning.

Downie, D., T. Slesnick, and J. Stenmark. **Math for Girls and Other Problem Solvers**. Berkeley, Calif.: University of California, Lawrence Hall of Science, 1981. 108p. Grades 1-6. Also available from Dale Seymour Publications.

This book includes mathematics activities to explore logical strategies, patterns, and estimation, to give practice in spatial visualization, and to explore careers.

Dutton, Wilbur H., and Ann Dutton. **Mathematics Children Use and Understand**. Mountain View, Calif.: Mayfield Publishing, 1991. 352p. Grades K-3. Also available from Dale Seymour Publications.

This book uses Jean Piaget's model of cognitive development and offers sequential, age-appropriate instruction. Contains scope and sequencing charts and evaluation techniques.

** Frank, Marjorie. **The Kids' Stuff Book of Math for the Primary Grades**, Grades 1-3, and **The Kids' Stuff Book of Math for the Middle Grades**, Grades 4-7. Nashville, Tenn.: Incentive Publications, 1988. Each, 240p.

These books contain high-interest activities for teaching number concepts, addition and subtraction, multiplication and division, fractions and decimals, geometry, problem solving, measurement, time, and money.

House, Peggy A., ed. **Providing Opportunities for the Mathematically Gifted, K-12**. Reston, Va.: National Council of Teachers of Mathematics, 1987. 108p. All grades. Also available from Dale Seymour Publications.

Exemplary programs for the mathematically gifted are illustrated. Includes a list of resources.

Johnson, D. W., R. T. Johnson, and E. J. Holubec. **Circles of Learning: Cooperation in the Classroom**. Ann Arbor, Mich.: Books on Demand, 1984. 128p. Also available from Dale Seymour Publications.

This guide to cooperative learning includes suggestions for implementing it in the classroom.

Laycock, Mary, and Peggy McLean. **Weaving Your Way from Arithmetic to Mathematics**. Hayward, Calif.: Activity Resources Company, 1993. 144p. Grades 2-8. Also available from Dale Seymour Publications.

This book discusses manipulatives and the NCTM standards. Includes assessment questions to help determine students' placement and contains comprehensive guidelines for developing math materials.

May, Lola J., and Larry Ecklund. **Unifix Teacher's Resource Book**. Rowley, Mass.: Didax Educational Resources, 1991. 66p.

** May, Lola J., and Shirley M. Frye. **Down to Earth Mathematics: Activities for Elementary Students**. Rowley, Mass.: Didax Educational Resources, 1995. 120p.
This eight-chapter book includes activities for students in grades K-6 as well as student objectives and teacher directions. Place value, addition and subtraction, multiplication and division, measurement, geometry, fractions, problem solving, and number sense are discussed.

National Council of Teachers of Mathematics.
The National Council has prepared many books that are available directly from them and other suppliers. Titles of particular interest include *Assessment in the Mathematics Classroom*, 248p.; *Calculators in Mathematics Education*, 256p.; *Curriculum and Evaluation Standards*, 258p.; *Implementing the K-8 Curriculum and Evaluation Standards*, 112p.; and *Professional Standards for Teaching Mathematics*, 196p. The *Addenda Series* includes *Kindergarten*, 24p.; *First Grade*, 24p.; *Second Grade*, 43p.; *Third Grade*, 32p.; *Fourth Grade*, 32p.; *Making Sense of Data*, 48p.; *Patterns*, 53p.; *Number Sense and Operations*, 56p.; and *Geometry and Spatial Sense*, 56p.

National Research Council. **Everybody Counts: A Report to the Nation on the Future of Mathematics Education**. 1989. 256p. Available from Dale Seymour Publications.
This report considers all aspects of mathematics education and outlines a national strategy for solving educational problems.

Parker, Ruth E. **Mathematical Power: Lessons from a Classroom**. Portsmouth, N.H.: Heinemann, 1993. 248p. Grades 4-6. Also available from Dale Seymour Publications.
Written from the perspective of a fifth-grade teacher, this book includes background and insights on NCTM reforms.

Payne, Joseph N. **Mathematics for the Young Child**. Reston, Va.: National Council of Teachers of Mathematics, 1990. 320p. Grades PreK-4. Also available from Dale Seymour Publications.
This publication suggests ways to present mathematics tasks, ask questions, and use manipulatives.

Richardson, Kathy. **Developing Number Concepts Using Unifix Cubes**. Reading, Mass.: Addison Wesley Longman, 1984. 300p. Also available from Didax Educational Resources.

Rowan, Thomas E., and Lorna J. Morrow, eds. **Implementing the K-8 Curriculum and Standards: Readings from the "Arithmetic Teacher."** Reston, Va.: National Council of Teachers of Mathematics, 1993. 172p. Also available from Dale Seymour Publications.
Articles are grouped by topic and include extensive references and an annotated bibliography.

Thiesen, Diane, and Margaret Matthias, eds. **The Wonderful World of Mathematics**. Reston, Va.: National Council of Teachers of Mathematics, 1993. 252p. Grades K-6. Also available from Dale Seymour Publications.

This annotated bibliography is divided into four categories: early number concepts, number extensions and connections, measurement, and geometry and spatial sense.

Thornton, Carol A., et al. **Teaching Mathematics to Students with Learning Disabilities**. Austin, Tex.: PRO-ED, 1994. 560p. Also available from Dale Seymour Publications.

This book helps instructors teach math more effectively to special-needs students.

Zaslavsky, Claudia. **Africa Counts: Number and Pattern in African Culture**. Chicago: Lawrence Hill Books, 1973. 336p. All grades. Also available from Dale Seymour Publications.

This comprehensive study covers important contributions to mathematics by African Americans.

Other Resources

(Manipulatives, games, sets, reproducibles, and computer diskettes)

** **Abacus**. Buffalo, N.Y.: SI Manufacturing Limited.

This product is available with four rods and ten rods and colored beads.

Abacus. Columbus, Ohio: Judy/Instructo.

This sturdy, four-wire wooden-bead abacus has 63 wooden beads and includes a teacher's guide.

Abacus, Bead Frame. Rowley, Mass.: Didax Educational Resources.

This 8¼-inch-by-7½-inch abacus has ten rods and can be used upright or on a tabletop.

Abacus, Slide. Rowley, Mass.: Didax Educational Resources.

In a nine-inch-by-six-inch frame, there are beads in five colors and useful horizontal and vertical number grids.

Activity Math. Reading, Mass.: Addison Wesley Longman, 1992. By Anne Bloomer and Phyllis Carlson. *Grades K-3* and *Grades 4-6*.

Each book is organized into ten strands to correlate with the NCTM standards. Contains blackline masters. Also available separately are *Activity Math Manipulatives Kits*.

Activity Math Kindergarten Kit. Palo Alto, Calif.: Dale Seymour Publications.

The kit contains 250 color beads, 500 snap cubes, 750 pattern blocks, 1,000 Link-Its, 25 laces, 250 pennies, 150 nickels, 150 dimes, 500 stacking chips, 500 craft sticks, a sorting and counting kit, and 400 color tiles in a 20-inch-by-20-inch-by-20-inch tote locker.

Activity Math Grades 1-3 Kit. Palo Alto, Calif.: Dale Seymour Publications.

The kit contains 600 base ten cubes, 300 base ten rods, 30 base ten flats, one base ten block, 1,000 Link-Its, 500 color tiles, 250 pennies, 150 nickels, 150 dimes, a dollar-bill money pack, a decimal-bar pack, 500 stacking chips, 500 craft sticks, 12 geoboards, 30 hundred boards, 500 snap cubes, 750 pattern blocks, 12 Cuisenaire-rod sets. The kit comes in a 20-inch-by-15-inch-by-22-inch tote locker.

Activity Math Grades 4-6 Kit. Palo Alto, Calif.: Dale Seymour Publications.

The kit contains 500 stacking chips, 24 geoboards, 300 two-color counters, 500 snap cubes, 750 pattern blocks, 600 base ten cubes, 300 base ten rods, 30 base ten flats, one base ten block, 12 protractors, 500 color tiles, a dollar-bill money pack, a decimal-bar pack. The kit comes in a 20-inch-by-15-inch-by-22-inch tote locker.

** **AIMS Laboratory Materials for Grades K-4**. Fresno, Calif.: AIMS Education Foundation.

A variety of materials are available separately or as classroom sets, including *Primer Balance, Gramstacker Mass Sets*, centimeter rulers, tape measures, flat meter sticks, metric-measuring-cup sets, metric spoon sets, liter boxes with lids, beakers, graduated cylinders, immersion thermometers, *teddy bear counters, astronaut counters, friendly bears*, and *flying astronauts*.

** **Base Ten Materials**. Palo Alto, Calif.: Dale Seymour Publications.

Base Ten Blocks are available in wood or plastic, as sets or as components. *Overhead Base Ten Block* comes as separate components or as a complete set in red and blue. *Base Ten Stamp Set* consists of four vinyl stamps to reproduce the 1,000-unit block, 100-unit flat, 10-unit rod, and single-unit cube. *Building Understanding with Base Ten Blocks*, by Mary Laycock, et al., Grades K-4, is a book of hands-on, reproducible lessons for solving computation problems. *The Place Value Connection*, by Diana A. D'Aboy, 136p., Grades 1-4, includes activities, games, and reproducible pages to be used with one to 100 charts. *The 1 to 100 Charts* are two charts, one pictorial and one with numerals, and include a miniguide for teaching place value and money. *The 1 to 1,000,000 Chart* displays the numeration system up to one million and includes a miniguide.

CaddyStack, Classroom Storage. Buffalo, N.Y.: SI Manufacturing Limited.

Colorful caddys are used for stacking and storing a variety of math materials, such as calculators, cubes, and pattern blocks.

CaddyStack Organizer, Calculator CaddyStack, Caddy Rack, Stacking Trays, and Storage Trays. Rowley, Mass.: Didax Educational Resources.

Individual containers and groups of plastic containers are available to store math manipulatives.

CountDown. New York: Voyager Company. By Margo Nanny and Robert Mohl. All grades. Also available from Dale Seymour Publications.

Macintosh-compatible CD-ROM with 16-page user's guide. Contains three games to explore operations, logic, and more.

** **Cuisenaire Rods**. White Plains, N.Y.: Cuisenaire Company of America, 1977.

The Cuisenaire Starter Set, available with plastic or wooden rods, comes with a self-sorting tray, the 160-page *Ideas for Cuisenaire Rods at the Primary Level*, and the 24-page *Learning with Cuisenaire Rods* teacher's guide. *Cuisenaire Rods Set* includes 74 plastic or wooden rods with books and a poster. *Six Trays of Cuisenaire*

Rods are available in wood or plastic with books. *Idea Book for Cuisenaire Rods at the Primary Level*, by Patricia S. Davidson, PreK-2, 164p., is available separately. *Student Activity Cards for Cuisenaire Rods*, by P. Davidson, A. Fair, and G. Galton, Grades 1-6, consists of 126 cards with games and activities across ten topic areas. *Picture Puzzles with Cuisenaire Rods*, by Patricia S. Davison and Jeffrey B. Sellon, Grades 1-6, is a reproducible 64-page puzzle book.

 A Day with Lola May Video Series. Available from Dale Seymour Publications and other distributors.

Complete set includes 15 videos with a teacher's guide. Each cassette is 20 minutes and includes suggestions for teachers in math classrooms. Components are also available separately. Videos include *The Meaning of Math*; *Ways to Motivate Students, Part I*; *Ways to Motivate Students, Part II*; *Models to Help You Teach*; *Strategies to Teach the Basic Facts*; *Trouble Spots: Addition and Subtraction*; *Trouble Spots: Multiplication*; *Trouble Spots: Division*; *Word Problems*; *Concept of Fractions*; *Operation of Fractions*; *Meaning of Decimals*; *Strategies of Problem Solving*; *Techniques of Calculators*; and *Estimation Skills*.

Early Math. Austin, Tex.: Steck-Vaughn Company.

In the complete set, there are 24 16- to 24-page workbooks on basic math skills and concepts. The *Readiness Set*, which comes with ten of each of the four titles, includes the workbooks *Readiness*, *Number Sense*, *Shapes*, and *Readiness for Problem Solving*. *Addition and Subtraction Set 1* includes the workbooks *Place Value to 100*, *Addition 0-5*, *Addition 6-10*, *Subtraction 1-10*, and *Mixed Operations*. *Addition and Subtraction Set 11* includes *Two-Digit Addition and Subtraction Without Regrouping*, *Two-Digit Addition with Regrouping*, *Place Value II*, *Two- and Three-Digit Addition*, *Two-Digit Subtraction with Regrouping*. *Time, Money, Measurement, Fractions, and Problem-Solving Set I* includes the workbooks *Time I*, *Money I*, *Measurement I*, *Fractions I*, and *Problem Solving I*. *Time, Money, Measurement, Fractions, and Problem-Solving Set II* includes workbooks *Time II*, *Money II*, *Measurement II*, *Fractions II*, and *Problem Solving II*. Answer keys are included.

** **Elementary School Mathematics: Teaching Developmentally**. 2d ed. White Plains, N.Y.: Longman, 1994. By John A. Van de Walle. 544p. Grades K-8. Also available from Dale Seymour Publications.

This second edition resource book encourages teachers to consider mathematics from the student's perspective. It includes references and blackline masters.

Explorations: A Hands-on Discovery Math Program. Reading, Mass.: Addison Wesley Longman.

This is an activity-based curriculum and comes with a variety of pieces. *Explorations for Early Childhood*, 224p., 48 blackline masters; *Explorations Grade 1 Math Program*, 322p. and 104 blackline masters; *Explorations Grade 1 Student Activity Book*; *Explorations Grade 2 Math Program*, 356p., 104 blackline masters; *Explorations Grade 2 Student Activity Book*. These also come as kits that include manipulatives.

** **Exploring Everyday Math: Ideas for Students, Teachers, and Parents**. Portsmouth, N.H.: Heinemann, 1993. By Maja Apelman and Julie King. 264p. Grades K-6. Also available from Dale Seymour Publications.

This book focuses on activities and everyday applications of math and includes reproducible recording sheets, sample letters to parents, and workshop suggestions.

Fall into Math and Science; Glide into Winter with Math and Science; and Spring into Math and Science. Fresno, Calif.: AIMS Education Foundation, Grades K-1.

The three books contain activities relating to holidays and the seasons and provide opportunities for graphing, counting, measurement, and patterning.

 Fizz and Martina Intermediate Video Kits. Watertown, Mass.: Tom Snyder Productions. Grades 3-6. Also available from Creative Publications.

Each kit contains a video, student workbooks, a teacher's guide, cards, and blackline masters. There are four math dilemmas per video. The titles include *Fizz and Martina at Blue Falls High; Fizz and Martina Conquer Project Sphinx; Fizz and Martina Do Hollywood;* and *2% Wiseguy, 98% Same Old Kid*.

 Hands-on Math: Computer Software and Manipulatives. Grover Beach, Calif.: Ventura Educational Systems. All grades. Available from Dale Seymour Publications.

These materials are divided into *Volumes 1, 2, 3* software and *Volumes 1, 2, 3* manipulatives. Volume 1 provides experience with number theory, creating math journals, place value, area, perimeter, fractions, problem solving, and visual thinking. Volume 2 explores probability, sorting, counting, patterns, symmetry, logical thinking, and place value. Volume 3 provides practice with multiples; prime numbers; arithmetic; number patterns; bar, line, and circle graphs; problem solving; line design; fractions; and equations. Software is provided on 3½-inch disk for Macintosh and comes with a teacher's guide and reproducible work sheets.

Hundreds Materials. Palo Alto, Calif.: Dale Seymour Publications.

Try It! Hundred Number Boards are riddles that are solved by following numerical directions using hundred boards. *Hundred Boards* come in sets of ten plastic-coated cardboard sheets with one-inch squares and can be used with *Link-Its*, which are plastic, open one-inch squares in four colors and which come with a 16-page instruction booklet. *Pad of 100 Charts* are usable 100-sheet pads.

Investigations in Number, Data, and Space. Palo Alto, Calif.: Dale Seymour Publications. Grades K-5.

This is a full math curriculum with lesson plans, materials, and assessment plans. Units can be purchased separately. Grades 3 and 4 were the first materials to become available in 1995 with other grades to follow. Typical units for Grade 3 include *From Paces to Feet*, which covers measuring and data; *Flips, Turns, and Area*, covering two-dimensional geometry; and *Fair Shares*, which covers fractions. Typical units for Grade 4 include *Arrays and Shares*, which covers multiplication and division; *Landmarks in the Thousands*, covering the number system; and *Changes Over Time*, which covers graphs. Student materials to support the program are available as kits or individual components.

It's the Thought That Counts. Palo Alto, Calif.: Dale Seymour Publications. By Lawrence Lowery, et al. 208p.

This book contains many math activities correlated to Piaget's stages of mental development and includes reproducible work sheets.

** K-2 Kit for Use with NCTM Addenda Series. Vernon Hills, Ill.: ETA.

The kit includes three NCTM books: *Kindergarten Book, First Grade Book, Second Grade Book*. Provides hands-on experiences with sorting materials, cubes, links, coins, tiles, dominoes, pattern blocks, geoboards, and hundred boards.

Letter Machine. Newport Beach, Calif.: Ellison Educational.

Ellison letter machines can be used to make math manipulatives out of such materials as construction paper, felt, pasteboard, laminated paper, fabric, and polyfoam. Different decorative dies are available for use with the machine.

LinkerCubes. Worth, Ill.: Creative Publications. Grades K-12.

These two-centimeter cubes comes in ten colors. They can be used to explore place value; investigate area, perimeter, and volume; and to solve problems. Also available are *LinkerCubes for the Overhead Projector*; the *LinkerCubes Sample*, which includes five buckets of LinkerCubes and the 16-page booklet, *Take Off with LinkerCubes*; *LinkerCubes Jobcards*, in a primary set for Grades 1-3 and an intermediate set for Grades 4-6; *LinkerCubes Jobcards Starter Sets* for primary or intermediate grades with a bucket of LinkerCubes; *Moving on with LinkerCubes*, a 128-page binder of reproducible problem-solving lessons; the *Moving on with LinkerCubes Starter Set*, which contains the binder and materials for four to eight students; *Hands-on LinkerCubes*, a 128-page binder filled with problem-solving activities; and the *Hands-on LinkerCubes Starter Set*, which includes the binder and enough materials for four to six students; *Primary Cooperative Problem Solving with Linker-Cubes*, Grades 1-3, by Ann Roper, 83 pages, includes reproducibles and problems and is available in Spanish or English and as a *Classroom Kit* that includes two buckets of LinkerCubes; *20 Thinking Questions for LinkerCubes: Grades 1-3*, by Kathryn Walker and Kelly Stewart, 112 pages, is available separately and as a *Classroom Kit* with manipulatives. All items may also be purchased as the *LinkerCubes Elementary School Kit*.

Manipulative Kits. Vernon Hills, Ill.: ETA.

Kits are available for kindergarten, first grade, second grade, and third and fourth grades. Depending on the grade level, these kits contain such items as sorting trays, coins, attribute blocks, clocks, PopCubes, sorting buttons, pattern blocks, Link 'N Learn, rocker balance, hundred boards, base ten units, and metric rulers. Each kit provides enough manipulatives for a whole class, and the price for the kit usually represents a 20 percent savings over buying the same number of items individually. Such items are also packaged as *Mathematical Discoveries for Early Childhood Activity Kit*, *Mathematical Discoveries for Young Children*, *Primary Math Manipulative Kit*, and *Intermediate Math Manipulative Kit*.

Math in Stride. Reading, Mass.: Addison Wesley Longman, 1980. By C. Clark, B. Y. Carter, and B. J. Sternberg. Grades 1-6.

This series involves usable workbooks and teacher sourcebooks with a blackline master pad. Also available is a *Math in Stride Assessment Program*.

Mathematics: Exploring Your World. Columbus, Ohio: Silver Burdett Ginn. By Ruth Champagne, Herbert Ginsburg, Carole Greenes, Larry Leutzinger, William Mckillip, Lucy Orfan, Fernand Prevost, Bruce Vogeli, Marianne Weber. Student texts and teacher editions, Grades K-4.

Problem solving is the focus of the program. Additional resources include *Achieving Higher Test Scores*, *Calculator Connection Cards*, *Celebrating Diversity* (poetry), *Multicultural Poster Package*, *Problem of the Day*, *Grade Level Manipulative Kits*, *Overhead Projector Manipulative Kits*, *Punch-Out Manipulatives*, and *Sets of Calculators* with cards and a teacher's guide. Also available is *Logo Geometry*, *Grades K-6*, with which students construct an understanding of shapes, angles, rotations, congruence, and other geometric concepts.

Mathematics Activities for Home Schooling with Unifix Cubes. Rowley, Mass.: Didax Educational Resources. By Don Balka.

This 64-page book is designed to be used by first- to fifth-grade children along with Unifix Cubes to reinforce patterning with numbers 0 to 100, measurement and estimation, addition and subtraction, mental math, fractions, area, and perimeter. An activities kit is also available and includes 100 Unifix Cubes, a black spinner, 1-100 board, a pattern board, a 1-10 stair board, and a set of Unifix Tens and Hundreds Cubes.

 ** **Mathematics Education Videotapes**. White Plains, N.Y.: Cuisenaire Company of America. By Marilyn Burns.

These comprehensive videos feature actual classroom lessons and include a teacher's guide. *Manipulatives*, Grades K-6, contains six 20-minute tapes available individually or as a set. Titles include *Base Ten Blocks, Pattern Blocks, Cuisenaire Rods, Color Tiles, Geoboards*, and *Six Models*. *Teaching for Understanding*, Grades K-6, is a set of three videotapes. The programs focus on place value, multiplication, and fractions. Each 20-minute tape comes with a teacher's guide. *Assessing Understanding*, Grades 2-8, is a set of three 20-minute videos and comes with a teacher's guide. Individual interviews with students show how to pose assessment questions, teach students to think through responses, probe students' reasoning, and determine their understanding.

** **Mathematics Their Way**. Reading, Mass.: Addison Wesley Longman, 1976. By Mary Baratta-Lorton. 416p. Grades K-2.

This teacher's guide is for teaching this popular program. Includes blackline masters. Also available is the *ETA Kit Designed for Math Their Way*, which provides the materials needed to concretely present math concepts in counting, sorting, patterning, graphing, measuring, operations, place value, and problem solving. Available separately are sorting buttons, number cubes, storage jars, junque boxes, a canvas graphing mat, and a graphing mat.

Number Power: A Cooperative Approach to Mathematics and Social Development. Reading, Mass.: Addison Wesley Longman, 1993. By L. Robertson, S. Regan, T. W. Contestable, and M. Freeman. Grades 2-6.

Each kit contains a teacher's resource book, usable group record sheets, manipulatives, and overhead transparencies. Each teacher's guide contains three units with eight to 12 lessons and blackline masters.

Opening Eyes to Mathematics. Salem, Oreg.: Math Learning Center.

This math curriculum is used in multiaged primary school classrooms and by third- and fourth-grade teachers. It contains three volumes of lessons, a teaching reference manual, a calendar extravaganza, overhead transparencies, and blackline masters. Also available is an *Opening Eyes to Mathematics Manipulative Kit*, which contains the manipulatives necessary for a class of 30 students.

Overhead Manipulatives in Action Binders. Birmingham, Ala.: The Re-Print Corporation. Grades K-6.

The *Primary Binder* uses Three Bear Attribute Counters, attribute blocks, the numbers one to 100, counters, base ten blocks, coins, pattern blocks, clock dials, and fraction circles and is suitable for K-3. It is also available as an *Overhead Kit* and includes the binder plus all the manipulatives required for a group of 13. The *Intermediate Binder, Grades 3-6*, uses base ten transparencies, hundred boards, counters, bills, coins, pattern blocks, geoboards, fraction squares, rainbow fraction tiles, and tangrams. It is also available as an *Overhead Kit* with the binder and manipulatives for 14.

Overhead Manipulatives Kit. Greensboro, N.C.: Carson-Dellosa Publishing.
This six-book kit includes *Using Manipulatives to Teach Mathematics (K-4)*, *Using Manipulatives to Teach Mathematics II (K-4)*, *Math Manipulatives for the Overhead (K-4)*, *More Math Manipulatives for the Overhead (K-4)*, *Making Math Manipulatives (K-5)*, and *Math Transparencies (All Ages)*. In addition to the books, the kit contains for the overhead: bear counters, clocks, fraction builders, fraction squares, fraction circles, attribute blocks, base ten blocks, bills, coins, color tiles, counters, pattern blocks, and tangrams.

Points of Departure Teacher's Guides. Rowley, Mass.: Didax Educational Resources.
Each 20-page booklet provides creative ideas for classroom activities using mathematics manipulatives. Materials are available as a set or individually. Titles include *Pattern Blocks, Fraction Pieces, Interlocking Cubes, Color Tiles, Base Ten Blocks, Attribute Blocks, Geoblocks, Geoboards*, and *Hundred Boards*.

Structuring Cooperative Learning. Edina, Minn.: Interaction Book Company, 1987. R. T. Johnson, D. W. Johnson, and E. J. Holubec, eds. 352p. All grades. Also available from Dale Seymour Publications.
This resource book includes articles on cooperative learning. Lessons include teaching plans and reproducible work sheets.

** **Thinking in Logo**. Reading, Mass.: Addison Wesley Longman, 1988. By Gini Shimabukuro. 272p. Grades K-3. Also available from Dale Seymour Publications.
This teacher's sourcebook contains blackline masters. *Turtle Math*, by Douglas H. Clements and Julie Sarama Meredith, Grades 3-6, includes 36 logo-based investigations. Available on disk for Macintosh, it includes a teacher's resource guide.

** **Third & Fourth Grade Kit for Use with NCTM Addenda Series**. Vernon Hills, Ill.: ETA.
This kit contains the NCTM *Third Grade Book* and *Fourth Grade Book*. Provides opportunities for investigation using measuring tools, PopCubes, pattern blocks, hundred boards, and cubes.

Under Construction: Beginning Math. Blacklick, Ohio: SRA/McGraw Hill. By Pam Schiller and Lynne Peterson. Grades PreK-1. The DLM Early Childhood Program.
The program's books, activities, and CD-ROM disks are available in Spanish and English. To support the program you need color tiles, attribute buttons, and multicubes, which are available separately from the same publisher.

** **Unifix Cube Materials**. Palo Alto, Calif.: Dale Seymour Publications.
Unifix Cubes, which come in ten colors, are available in boxes of 100, 500, or 1,000. *Unifix Operation Grid, Tray and Number Card Set* has a number card with one to 100 on one side and a table square on the reverse. *Pattern Building Underlay Cards* are for use with the Operational Grid. *Unifix Operational Grid* is a plastic tray and grid with 100 recesses to hold Unifix Cubes. *Unifix 1-10 Stair* allows students to place Unifix Cubes in vertical grooves to total the value printed on the top. *Unifix Hundreds, Tens, and Ones Place Value Trays* come in five-tray sets and contain three grooves, each of which holds nine Unifix Cubes. *Unifix Mathematics Activities:*

Place Value and Computation Through Millions, by Don Balka, Grades 4-6, is a 56-page book that includes blackline masters. It helps students learn about number systems, statistics, fractions, whole number computation, and estimation. *Mathematics with Cubes*, by Janine Blinko and Noel Graham, is a 64-page book with problem-solving activities for use with Unifix Cubes, SnapCubes, or Multilink Cubes.

✷✷ Unifix Cube Materials. Rowley, Mass.: Didax Educational Resources.

Many pieces are available, including *Unifix Operational Grid and Tray* to hold *Unifix Cubes*; *Unifix Pattern Building Underlay Cards*; *Unifix Value Cards*; *Unifix Number Group Underlay Cards*; *My First Unifix Counting Book*; *Unifix Cubes for Pattern Building*; *Unifix Activity Cards*; *Unifix 1-5 Stair*; *Unifix 1-10 Stair*; *Unifix Number Indicators*; *Unifix Inset Pattern Boards*; *Unifix Dual Number Board*; *Unifix 20-100 Notation Cards*; *Unifix 10 x 10 Number Tray*; *Unifix Operational Grid, Tray and Number Card Set*; *Unifix 1-100 Number Tiles*; *Unifix Window Markers*; *Unifix Underlay Number Cards*; *Unifix Building to 100 Board*; *Unifix Counting Ladder*; *Unifix Cubes for the Overhead Projector*; *Unifix One-Ten and Ones Tray*; *Unifix Number Cards*; *Unifix Hundreds, Tens, and Ones Place Value Tray*; *Unifix Tens and Hundreds Cubes*; *Unifix Five-Tens and Ones Tray*; *Unifix Gummed Sheets*; *Unifix Wax Crayons*; *Unifix 100 Track*; *Unifix Multiplication and Division Markers*; *Unifix Rod Stamps Actual Cube Size*; *Unifix Rod Stamps Half Cube Size*; *Unifix Number and Group Making Stamps*; *Unifix Mathematics Manipulative Kit Preschool-K*; *Unifix Mathematics Manipulative Kit, Grades 1-2*; *Unifix Mathematics Manipulative Kit, Grades 3-4*; *Beginning Mathematics with Unifix Kit*; *Unifix Foundation Kit*; *Unifix Pattern Activity Kit Preschool*; *Unifix Extension Kit*; *Unifix Volume and Area Activities Kit*; *Unifix Assembly Grids and Retaining Frames*; *Unifix Basic Mathematics Kit*; and *Unifix Mathematics Home Helper*.

✷✷ Unifix Cube Materials. Birmingham, Ala.: The Re-Print Corporation. Grades K-5.

A variety of Unifix materials are available, including *Unifix Cubes*, *Unifix 1-10 Value Boats*, *Unifix 1-10 Stair*, and *Unifix Mathematics Activities—Book 1*, by Don Balka, PreK-2; *Unifix Mathematics Activities Book 2*, Grades K-4; *Developing Number Concepts Using Unifix Cubes*, by Kathy Richardson; *Unifix Teacher's Resource Book*, by Lola May and Larry Ecklund, 68p.; *My First Unifix Counting Book*, by Nixie Taverner for beginners; *Unifix Operational Grid and Tray*, *Unifix Pattern Building Underlay Cards*, *Unifix Hundreds, Tens, and Ones Place Value Tray*; *Unifix Number Indicators*; *Unifix Foundation Kit*; *Unifix Inset Pattern Boards*; *Unifix Basic Mathematics Kit*; *Unifix Mathematics Home Helper*; and *Beginning Mathematics with Unifix Kit*.

✷✷ Unifix Mathematics Activities Books. Rowley, Mass.: Didax Educational Resources. By Don Balka.

Book 1, PreK-2, includes precounting, early counting, and additional experiences. *Book 2*, Grades K-4, includes addition, subtraction, place value, multiplication, fractions, measurement, and statistics. *Book 3*, Grades 4-8, covers volume, area, and perimeter, and *Book 4*, Grades 3-6, covers place value and computation through millions.

Wooden Cubes. Palo Alto, Calif.: Dale Seymour Publications.

Cubes are useful for many activities. Plain or colored, they are available in sets of 100 in one-inch or two-centimeter sizes. *Color Cube Task Cards*, Grades K-3, provide practice with models.

CHAPTER 15

ADDRESSES OF PUBLISHERS AND SUPPLIERS

Most suppliers welcome your interest and your questions. Catalogs are expensive, but most companies will send a free catalog on request, especially if the request is made on school letterhead. Many companies also have local or regional representatives and distributors who can provide quick service and answer questions. If you write for a catalog, you might also ask for the name, address, and phone number of the closest distributor or representative.

Activity Resources Company, Inc.
P.O. Box 4875
20655 Hathaway Avenue
Hayward, CA 94541
(510) 782-1300

Addison Wesley Longman, Inc.
1 Jacob Way
Reading, MA 01867
(800) 447-2226

AIMS Education Foundation
P.O. Box 8120
Fresno, CA 93747-8120
(209) 255-4094

Benjamin/Cummings Publishing Co.
2725 Sand Hill Road
Menlo Park, CA 94025-7019
(415) 854-0300

Books on Demand
Division of UMI
300 N. Zeeb Road
Ann Arbor, MI 48106-1346
(800) 521-0600

Borenson & Associates
P.O. Box 3328
Allentown, PA 18106
(610) 398-6908

Broderbund Software, Inc.
500 Redwood Boulevard
Novato, CA 94948-6121
(800) 521-6263

Carson-Dellosa Publishing Company, Inc.
P.O. Box 35665
Greensboro, NC 27425
(800) 321-0943

Chronicle Books
275 Fifth Street
San Francisco, CA 94103
(415) 777-7240

Creative Publications
5623 W. 115th Street
Worth, IL 60482-9931
(800) 624-0822

Creative Wonders/Electronic Arts
1450 Fashion Island Boulevard
San Mateo, CA 94404
(800) 244-4525 (orders)
(415) 513-7226

Critical Thinking Press & Software
P.O. Box 448
Pacific Grove, CA 93950-0448
(408) 393-3288

Crown Books for Young Readers
Division of Random House, Inc.
201 E. 50th Street
New York, NY 10022
(800) 726-0600

Cuisenaire Company of America, Inc.
P.O. Box 5026
White Plains, NY 10602-5026
(800) 872-1100

Dale Seymour Publications
P.O. Box 5026
White Plains, NY 10602-5026
(800) 872-1100

Davidson and Associates, Inc.
19840 Pioneer Avenue
Torrance, CA 90503
(800) 545-7677

Delmar Publishers
P.O. Box 15015
Albany, NY 12212-5015
(518) 464-3500

Didax Educational Resources
395 Main Street
Rowley, MA 01969
(800) 458-0024

Dutton
375 Hudson Street
New York, NY 10014
(212) 366-2600

Educational Insights, Inc.
16941 Keegan Avenue
Carson, CA 90746
(800) 933-3277

Egghead Software
22011 S.E. 51st Street
Issaquah, WA 98027-7299
(800) 344-4323

Ellison Educational
P.O. Box 8209
Newport Beach, CA 92658-8209
(800) 253-2238

ETA
620 Lakeview Parkway
Vernon Hills, IL 60061
(800) 445-5985

Fearon Teacher Aids
A Judy/Instructo Company
4350 Equity Drive
Columbus, OH 43216
(800) 876-5507

Fidelity Products Company
5601 International Parkway
P.O. Box 155
Minneapolis, MN 55440-0155
(800) 326-7555

Gamco Industries, Inc.
Subsidiary of Siboney Corporation
P.O. Box 1911
Big Spring, TX 79721
(800) 351-1404

Glenwood Publications
540 Glenwood Lane
East Meadow, NY 11554
(516) 536-7846

Good Apple, Inc.
4350 Equity Drive
P.O. Box 2649
Columbus, OH 43216
(800) 435-7234

Greenwillow Books
1350 Avenue of the Americas
New York, NY 10019
(800) 843-9289

Harcourt Brace & Company
525 B Street, Suite 1900
San Diego, CA 92101
(619) 699-6707

Hartley Courseware, Inc.
Division of Jostens Learning Corporation
9920 Pacific Heights Boulevard, #500
San Diego, CA 92121-4334
(800) 247-1380

Heinemann
361 Hanover Street
Portsmouth, NH 03801-3912
(800) 541-2086

Houghton Mifflin Company
222 Berkeley Street
Boston, MA 02116-3764
(617) 351-5000

Incentive Publications
3835 Cleghorn Avenue
Nashville, TN 37215
(800) 431-2830

Institute for Math Mania
P.O. Box 910
Montpelier, VT 05601-0910
(800) 686-3725

Interact
1825 Gillespie Way, #101
El Cajon, CA 92020
(619) 448-1474

Interaction Book Company
7208 Cornelia Drive
Edina, MN 55435
(612) 831-9500

Judy/Instructo
4350 Equity Drive
P.O. Box 2649
Columbus, OH 43216
(800) 526-9907

Kaidy Educational Resources
P.O. Box 831853
Richardson, TX 75083-1853
(214) 234-6161

Lawrence Erlbaum Associates
10 Industrial Avenue
Mahwah, NJ 07430-2262
(800) 926-6579

Lawrence Hall of Science
University of California
Berkeley, CA 94720
(510) 642-1929

Lawrence Hill Books
814 N. Franklin Street, 2nd Floor
Chicago, IL 60610
(800) 888-4741

The Learning Company
6493 Kaiser Drive
Fremont, CA 94555
(800) 852-2255

Learning Links, Inc.
2300 Marcus Avenue
Dept. 94
New Hyde Park, NY 11042
(800) 724-2616

Learning Resources, Inc.
675 Heathrow Drive
Lincolnshire, IL 60069
(800) 222-3909

Legacy Software
8521 Reseda Boulevard
Northridge, CA 91324-4629
(800) 532-7692

Little, Brown & Company
Time & Life Building
1271 Avenue of the Americas
New York, NY 10020
(212) 522-8700

Longman Publishing Group
Division of Addison Wesley Longman, Inc.
The Longman Building
10 Bank Street
White Plains, NY 10606-1951
(800) 862-7778

Lothrop, Lee & Shepard Books
Division of William Morrow & Co., Inc.
1350 Avenue of the Americas
New York, NY 10019
(800) 843-9389

M. Evans and Company, Inc.
216 E. 49th Street
New York, NY 10017-1502
(212) 688-2810

Marilyn Burns Education Associates
150 Gate 5 Road, Suite 101
Sausalito, CA 94965
(800) 868-9092

Math Learning Center
P.O. Box 3226
Salem, OR 97302
(503) 370-8130

Mayfield Publishing Company
1280 Villa Street
Mountain View, CA 94041
(800) 433-1279

MECC/Softkey International Inc.
6160 Summit Drive North
Minneapolis, MN 55430
(800) 685-6322

MESD Press
11611 N.E. Ainsworth Circle
Portland, OR 97220
(503) 255-1841

Millbrook Press
2 Old New Milford Road
Brookfield, CT 06804
(203) 740-2220

MindPlay
Division of Methods and Solutions, Inc.
160 W. Fort Lowell Boulevard
Tuscon, AZ 85705-3812
(800) 221-7911

NASCO
901 Janesville Avenue
P.O. Box 901
Fort Atkinson, WI 53538-0901
(414) 563-2446

National Council of Teachers of Mathematics
1906 Association Drive
Reston, VA 22091
(800) 235-7566

NES Arnold, Inc.
899 H Airport Park Road
Glen Burnie, MD 21061-2557
(410) 553-9700

Optimum Resources
P.O. Box 23317
Hilton Head, SC 29925
(800) 327-1473

Oriental Trading Company, Inc.
P.O. Box 3407
Omaha, NE 68103-0407
(800) 228-2269

Pantheon Books
201 E. 50th Street, 25th Floor
New York, NY 10022
(800) 726-0600

Philomel Books
200 Madison Avenue
New York, NY 10016
(212) 951-8700

PlayFair Toys
P.O. Box 18210
Boulder, CO 80308
(800) 824-7255

Polydron USA, Inc.
2750 S. Harbor Boulevard, Suite C
Santa Ana, CA 92704
(800) 452-9978

PRO-ED
8700 Shoal Creek Boulevard
Austin, TX 78757-6897
(512) 451-3246

The Putnam Berkley Group
200 Madison Avenue
New York, NY 10016
(212) 951-8700

The Re-Print Corporation
P.O. Box 830677
Birmingham, AL 35283
(800) 248-9171

Rigby
P.O. Box 797
Crystal Lake, IL 60039-0797
(800) 822-8661

Scholastic Inc.
411 Lafayette
New York, NY 10003
(800) 325-6149

SI Manufacturing Limited
Olympic Towers, Suite 200
300 Pearl Street
Buffalo, NY 14202
(716) 842-6027

Silver Burdett Ginn
4350 Equity Drive
Columbus, OH 43228
(800) 848-9500

SRA/McGraw Hill
37 North Avenue
Norwalk, CT 06851
(203) 849-2866

Steck-Vaughn Company
P.O. Box 26015
Austin, TX 78755
(512) 343-8227

Stokes Publishing Company
P.O. Box 14401
Atlanta, GA 30324
(404) 365-8975

Teachers College Press
1234 Amsterdam Avenue
New York, NY 10027
(212) 678-3929

Tin Man Press
P.O. Box 219
Stenwood, WA 98292
(800) 676-0459

Tom Snyder Productions
80 Coolidge Hill Road
Watertown, MA 02172-2817
(800) 342-0236

Tricon Publishing
P.O. Box 146
Mount Pleasant, MI 48804
FAX (517) 773-5894

Troll Learn & Play
100 Corporate Drive
Mahwah, NJ 07430
(800) 929-8765

U.S. Toy Company, Inc.
1227 E. 119th Street
Grandview, MO 64030
(800) 255-6124

The Voyager Company
578 Broadway, Suite 406
New York, NY 10012
(800) 446-2001

William Morrow & Company, Inc.
Subsidary of Hearst Corporation
1350 Avenue of the Americas
New York, NY 10019
(800) 843-9389

Workman Publishing Company
708 Broadway
New York, NY 10003
(800) 722-7202

The Wright Group
19201 120th Avenue NE
Bothell, WA 98011-9512
(800) 523-2371

SUBJECT INDEX

ABOUT THE AUTHOR

PHYLLIS J. PERRY has worked as a teacher, an elementary school principal, a district curriculum specialist, a supervisor of student teachers, and as a director of talented and gifted education. She is the author of more than two dozen books for children and teachers, including five "First Books" for Franklin Watts and the "Literature Bridges to Science Series" for Teacher Ideas Press.

Dr. Perry received her undergraduate degree from the University of California at Berkeley and her doctorate from the University of Colorado in Boulder. She now devotes full time to writing and lives with her husband, David, in Boulder, Colorado.

from **Teacher Ideas Press**

Math Through Children's Literature: Making the NCTM Standards Come Alive
Kathryn L. Braddon, Nancy J. Hall, and Dale Taylor

Launch children into the world of mathematical literacy with books that give them the opportunity to experience the joy of math through their **own** understanding. Following the NCTM Standards, these literature activities are designed around an integrated reading process that caputres a child's interest and brings math to life. **Grades 1–6**.
xviii, 218p. 8½x11 paper ISBN 0-87287-932-1

Chances Are: Hands-on Activities in Probability and Statistics, Grades 3–7
Sheila Dolgowich, Helen M. Lounsbury, and Barry G. Muldoon

Fun with statistics? Chances are *yes* with this new resource! Through simple and enjoyable learning experiences, this hands-on activity book introduces students to a variety of mathematical concepts that are directly tied to the NCTM Standards. A comprehensive, easy-to-use teacher guide; reproducible activity sheets; and manipulatives accompany each activity. **Grades 3–7**. (*Great for the multiage classroom.*)
xviii, 125p. 8½x11 paper ISBN 1-56308-314-0

Science Through Children's Literature: An Integrated Approach
Carol M. Butzow and John W. Butzow

This best-seller provides instructional units that integrate all areas of the curriculum and serve as models to educators at all levels. Adopted by schools of education nationwide, it features more than 30 outstanding children's fiction books that are rich in scientific concepts yet equally well known for their strong story lines and universal appeal. **Grades K–3**.
xviii, 234p. 8½x11 paper ISBN 0-87287-667-5

Practical Portfolios: Reading, Writing, Math, and Life Skills, Grades 3–6
Susan B. Mundell and Karen DeLario

Build skills, reinforce learning, communicate achievements, and prepare students for future challenges with practical portfolios. You can use this material in subjects ranging from reading, writing, math, and life skills to cooperative group work, interviewing, and career awareness. A great way to invest students with responsibility and to involve parents in the educational process. **Grades 3–6**.
vii, 149p. 8½x11 paper ISBN 1-56308-197-0

Glues, Brews, and Goos: Recipes and Formulas for Almost Any Classroom Project
Diana F. Marks

Pulling together hundreds of practical, easy recipes and formulas for classroom projects—from paints and salt map mixtures to volcanic actions—these kid-tested projects make learning authentic and enjoyable. All projects use ingredients that are easy to find and processes that are up-to-date. Tips on when, why, and how to use these terrific concoctions are also included. **Grades K–6**.
xvi, 179p. 8½x11 paper ISBN 1-56308-362-0

For a FREE catalog or to order any of our titles, please contact:
Teacher Ideas Press
Dept. B24 • P.O. Box 6633 • Englewood, CO 80155-6633
Phone: 1-800-237-6124 • Fax: 303-220-8843 • E-mail: lu-books@lu.com

www.ingramcontent.com/pod-product-compliance
Ingram Content Group UK Ltd.
Pitfield, Milton Keynes, MK11 3LW, UK
UKHW050147280225
455689UK00007B/93